T0296040

"This is a timely and important book that examines the development and implications of gig work. Technological change is impacting on how, where and when work takes place, under what conditions, and how it is organised and remunerated. The algorithmic management processes supporting gig work are being applied to the conventional workplace and working arrangements. The relevance and significance of this book extends beyond the online economy."

John Burgess, Professor of Human Resource Management in the School of Management, RMIT University

"This book is a must read for everyone interested in HRM in the platform-enabled gig economy. Besides addressing definitional questions, it touches upon important puzzles that characterize online labor platforms, including: algorithmic management, multi-party working relationships, and gig worker experiences."

Dr Jeroen Meijerink, Assistant Professor of Human Resource Management, University of Twente, The Netherlands

"This authoritative, wide-ranging and critical book is essential reading for anyone interested in work in the gig economy. The authors provide key insights on gig work and algorithmic management, showing convincingly how these challenge our current understanding of working relationships, job quality and people management. I highly recommend it."

Professor Anne Keegan, University College Dublin, Ireland

Work in the Gig Economy

Throughout the last decade, the "gig economy" has emerged as one of the most significant developments in the world of work. As a novel, hyper-flexible form of labour, gig work features a uniquely fragmented working arrangement wherein independent workers partner with digital platform organisations to provide a range of on-demand services to customers.

Work in the Gig Economy: A Research Overview provides a concise overview to the key themes and debate that encompass the gig economy literature. It covers five core themes: an introduction to gig work; classification issues; the role of technology; the experiences of gig workers; and the future of gig work. As an emerging and diverse research field, contributions stem from an array of perspectives including psychology, sociology, human resource management, legal studies, and technology management. The chapters synthesise the most prominent insights into this emerging field, key thinking on the complex relationships and conditions found in gig work, and the most significant issues to be addressed as the gig economy continues to develop.

A critical introduction for students, scholars, and reflective professionals and policymakers, this book provides much needed direction through the rapidly growing and expansive body of research on work in the gig economy.

James Duggan is Assistant Professor in Management at the School of Business, Maynooth University.

Anthony McDonnell is Full Professor of Human Resource Management, Head of the Department of Management and Marketing, and Co-director of the HR Research Centre at the Cork University Business School, University College Cork.

Ultan Sherman is Lecturer in Human Resource Management at Cork University Business School, University College Cork.

Ronan Carbery is Senior Lecturer in Management at Cork University Business School and Co-director of the HR Research Centre at University College Cork.

State of the Art in Business Research
Series Editor: Geoffrey Wood

Recent advances in theory, methods and applied knowledge (alongside structural changes in the global economic ecosystem) have presented researchers with challenges in seeking to stay abreast of their fields and navigate new scholarly terrains.

State of the Art in Business Research presents shortform books which provide an expert map to guide readers through new and rapidly evolving areas of research. Each title will provide an overview of the area, a guide to the key literature and theories and time-saving summaries of how theory interacts with practice.

As a collection, these books provide a library of theoretical and conceptual insights, and exposure to novel research tools and applied knowledge, that aid and facilitate in defining the state of the art, as a foundation stone for a new generation of research.

Public Management
A Research Overview
Tom Entwistle

Philosophy and Management Studies
A Research Overview
Raza Mir and Michelle Greenwood

Work in the Gig Economy
A Research Overview
James Duggan, Anthony McDonnell, Ultan Sherman, and Ronan Carbery

For more information about this series, please visit: www.routledge.com/State-of-the-Art-in-Business-Research/book-series/START

Work in the Gig Economy

A Research Overview

James Duggan, Anthony McDonnell, Ultan Sherman, and Ronan Carbery

LONDON AND NEW YORK

First published 2022
by Routledge
2 Park Square, Milton Park, Abingdon, Oxon OX14 4RN

and by Routledge
605 Third Avenue, New York, NY 10158

Routledge is an imprint of the Taylor & Francis Group, an informa business

British Library Cataloguing-in-Publication Data
A catalogue record for this book is available from the British Library

Library of Congress Cataloging-in-Publication Data
Names: Duggan, James, 1994- author.
Title: Work in the gig economy: a research overview/James Duggan, Anthony McDonnell, Ultan Sherman & Ronan Carbery.
Description: Abingdon, Oxon; New York, NY: Routledge, 2022. | Series: State of the art in business research | Includes bibliographical references and index.
Identifiers: LCCN 2021013369 (print) | LCCN 2021013370 (ebook)
Subjects: LCSH: Temporary employment. | Part-time employment. | Contractors.
Classification: LCC HD5854 .D84 2022 (print) | LCC HD5854 (ebook) | DDC 331.25/729–dc23
LC record available at https://lccn.loc.gov/2021013369
LC ebook record available at https://lccn.loc.gov/2021013370

ISBN: 978-0-367-36792-3 (hbk)
ISBN: 978-1-032-07526-6 (pbk)
ISBN: 978-0-429-35148-8 (ebk)

DOI: 10.4324/9780429351488

Typeset in Times New Roman
by Deanta Global Publishing Services, Chennai, India

Contents

Illustrations

Figures

Table

About the authors

James Duggan (PhD, MSc, BA) is Assistant Professor in Management at the School of Business, Maynooth University. With a background in new media and technology, James' research has been funded by the Irish Research Council and examines the fragmented nature of working relationships in the global gig economy. In particular, his research focuses on the role of algorithmic management in shaping the experiences of app-based gig workers. James' research has been published in *Human Resource Management Journal* and has been presented at several international conferences, including the Academy of Management Annual Meeting, the Academy of Management's Human Resource International Conference, and the European Human Resource Development Conference.

Twitter: @JamesDuggan01

Anthony McDonnell (PhD, BBS, MCIPD) is Full Professor of Human Resource Management, Head of the Department of Management and Marketing, and Co-director of the HR Research Centre at the Cork University Business School (CUBS), University College Cork. He has held appointments at Queen's University Belfast, University of South Australia, and University of Newcastle (Australia). His research has been funded by the Australian and Irish Research Councils and Ireland Canada University Foundation. He has an extensive publication record in the leading international journals including the *Journal of World Business, Human Resource Management (US), Human Relations, Industrial and Labor Relations Review, International Journal of Human Resource Management, Management International Review, and Human Resource Management Journal.*

Twitter: @amcdonnell_hrm

Ultan Sherman (BA, MBS, PhD, CPsychol, PsSI) lectures in Organisational Behaviour and Human Resource Management at Cork University Business

School, University College Cork. His research interests lie broadly in the relationship between work and psychology with specific focus on the psychological contract. His research has been published in leading international journals such as *Group & Organization Management, International Journal of Human Resource Management, European Journal of Work and Organizational Psychology*, and *Human Resource Management Journal*. A chartered psychologist with The Psychological Society of Ireland, Ultan has worked with major organisations in the areas of employee development, selection, and team dynamics.

Twitter: @ultansherman

Ronan Carbery (PhD, BComm, MCIPD) is Senior Lecturer in Management at Cork University Business School and Co-director of the HR Research Centre at University College Cork. He is co-editor of the *European Journal of Training and Development* and serves as an editorial advisory board member on *Human Resource Management Journal, Human Resource Development Quarterly*, and *Human Resource Development International*. He has co-edited a number of leading texts including *Human Resource Management* (2019) and *Human Resource Development: A Concise Introduction* (2015).

Twitter: @RonanCarbery

Acknowledgements

James
To my family, for your constant love and support.

Anthony
To the most important people – Therese, Tess, and Antonia

Ultan
To Fiona, Rachel, and Ted

Ronan
To Michelle and Julie

1 Work in the gig economy: an introduction[1]

Introduction

The gig economy has emerged as a much-discussed phenomenon across the world. Definitions of what represents the gig economy vary from incorporating all non-traditional and less structured work arrangements to a more specific focus on work performed via online platforms and crowdsourcing marketplaces. As such, Upwork, Uber, Lfyt, TaskRabbit, Fiverr, Just Eat, Airtasker, Amazon Mechanical Turk, Deliveroo, and Freelancer are often seen as key examples of organisations in the gig economy.

This book critically reviews research on work in the gig economy. More specifically, our focus is on gig work forms that are mediated via digital platform organisations. The book's aim is to provide readers with a critical summary of the key themes and debates that encompass the gig economy literature. In addition, we propose a series of future research avenues that we argue as having great importance in better understanding the nature of gig work. We draw primarily from scholarly publications over the last decade which encompass work from multiple disciplinary perspectives including the sociology of work, industrial relations, human resource management, work and organisational psychology, and technology management. Accordingly, this book is likely to hold appeal to students, scholars, and professionals seeking a comprehensive yet succinct overview of research on "gig work."

This first chapter tracks the emergence of the gig economy and accompanying working arrangements throughout the last decade. Specifically, we discuss the origins of the gig economy and account for its rapid growth as a widely recognised umbrella term associated with several multinational platform organisations and their associated working configurations. Additionally, this chapter also provides important background information and context for the specific issues considered throughout the book, where

DOI: 10.4324/9780429351488-1

the most controversial and pervasive aspects of gig work will be critically reviewed.

Key chapter takeaways

- The gig economy and its accompanying work forms have emerged as a significant disruptor to traditional understandings of work and employment.
- The gig economy continues to grow steadily but at the time of writing remains a relatively small component of the overall labour market.
- Gig work is not homogenous and instead represents a diverse economy built upon digital infrastructures that connect independent workers with clients or customers (i.e. requestors).
- Scholarly research on gig work spans multiple disciplines, but several ongoing key issues and themes relating to worker classification, technological disruption, and workers' experiences are common across literature.
- Empirical research on gig work remains in its infancy but is currently receiving increasing interest from scholars.

Introducing the gig economy

Over the past decade, the gig economy has been attracting both significant attention and controversy in the world of work. Broadly defined as an economic system that uses online platforms to digitally connect on-demand, freelance workers with requesters (i.e. customers or clients) to perform fixed-term tasks (Kuhn & Maleki, 2017), the gig economy embraces the information and connectivity properties enabled by modern technology to build service-providing digital infrastructures (Cennamo, 2019). The gig economy takes on many forms (c.f. Duggan et al., 2020; Howcroft & Bergvall-Kareborn, 2019) and operates across several sectors. For example, typical offerings that we regularly associate with the gig economy include on-demand services in local markets, such as transportation with Uber or Lyft, food delivery with Deliveroo or Uber Eats, and housekeeping and repair services with Handy (Smith & Leberstein, 2015). The gig economy also encapsulates remote, computer-based crowdwork companies, such as Fiverr and Amazon Mechanical Turk, where the services offered may range from translation to transcription to graphic design, and beyond (Howcroft & Bergvall-Kareborn, 2019). Perhaps to a lesser extent, capital platform organisations such as Airbnb and Etsy are sometimes also included as part of the gig economy, wherein individuals may sell goods or lease assets on platforms (Duggan et al., 2020).

Given the wide-ranging scope of services on offer and platform organisations available, the proliferation of the gig economy holds potentially noteworthy consequences for the world of work across the globe. In many cases, the tasks, or "gigs," to be completed by workers are simply components of formerly full-time roles held by taxi drivers, couriers, translators, secretaries, and so on, that have been fragmented into discrete tasks and made available on a precarious, often poorly paid task-by-task basis (Smith & Leberstein, 2015). However, when these and similar tasks are available as part of the gig economy, the outcome is that many gig workers must competitively strive to make a living by combining multiple short-term tasks, devoid of commitment and with piece-rate payments, which makes the realisation of a stable income difficult. Thus, it is not surprising that gig work, platform organisations, and individuals operating in this domain continue to receive such extensive attention from scholars, policymakers, governments, and media organisations (McGaughey, 2018). While parts of the gig economy involve high-skilled work, much of the focus appears on what traditionally are low-skilled jobs. However, the COVID-19 pandemic may reshape the public discourse on what essential work encompasses. The pandemic has seen key segments of the gig economy – for example, delivery drivers and couriers – being classified as essential workers across many economies. It also highlights the difficult situation so many gig workers are faced with in terms of their lack of job security in such crisis times. Many have been hit with loss of earnings and lack of sick leave.

Understanding gig workers

Classified as independent contractors in almost all cases, gig workers are purportedly granted the opportunity to "be your own boss" – essentially, the promise of freedom to work independently by controlling most aspects of the work, from scheduling to selecting tasks (Jabagi et al., 2019). For platform organisations, the avoidance of the "employee" label in classifying gig workers is of significant strategic importance in removing the need for, among other things, potential overtime payments, union organisation, payroll taxes, and unemployment benefits (Frost, 2017). In fact, gig work is characterised by such intense precarity, anonymity, and hyper-flexibility that most workers never actually meet their "employer" or any representative of the platform organisation, having landed their roles through online-only applications and a speedy onboarding process, with, in most cases, no formal training (Barley et al., 2017). However, while gig workers do not hold a legal employment relationship with the platform organisations for whom they work, a complex multi-party working relationship instead exists between the worker, platform organisation, and requester (Duggan et al.,

2020). By reshaping almost all of the conventions and norms that accompany traditional employment, the reimagined dynamic exchange agreement found in gig work subsequently creates various interdependencies and power dynamics between the parties involved (Meijerink & Keegan, 2019).

The precise nature of these interdependencies and power dynamics are a common source of debate across the literature. This is because platform organisations are known, in part at least, to utilise questionable and controversial practices in managing gig workers. Specifically, it is widely claimed that many platform organisations satisfy legal criteria to meet independent contractor status for gig workers, while simultaneously exerting significant levels of managerial control and surveillance over gig workforces (Shapiro, 2017; Norlander et al., 2021). Research has consistently addressed and supported this claim, suggesting that much of the autonomy afforded to these apparently independent gig workers is merely nominal, existing to attract workers to the platform and to fulfil legal criteria (Meijerink & Keegan, 2019; Wood et al., 2019). Instead, the reality of the working arrangement appears to be one where platform organisations attempt to avoid giving direct commands to workers, which may indicate the existence of an employment relationship, while simultaneously exerting significant control over most labour processes via the use of algorithmic technologies and punishing workers who fail to meet strict performance criteria (Duggan et al., 2020; Wu et al., 2019). The independent contractor status has been subject to several legal challenges across many countries, with decisions of the courts variable in respect to whether these workers should be classified as employees or not.

The emergence of the gig economy

During the global economic crisis of 2008, the nature of work and employment transformed dramatically. Working arrangements around the globe became, and have continued to become, more fragmented and precarious (Friedman, 2014). For example, we may naturally assume that the organisations whom we pay for services also employ the individuals or agents delivering the services being offered. However, essential duties within organisations are increasingly being carried out by contractors or temporary workers beyond the core boundaries of the firm, meaning such an assumption is increasingly challenged. This trend is part of what Weil (2017) describes as an increasingly fissured workplace, where organisations have sought to "outsource" a multitude of work activities in efforts to improve financial performance.

While this may prove to be a strategic activity for organisations, the fissured workplace undoubtedly creates complex new challenges for workers, potentially leaving many without stable income, career paths, or a safe working environment (Weil, 2017). Yet, for many, navigating this workplace has become the norm. In line with wider precarious working trends that are seeing a shift away from conventional working arrangements and the protections that accompany life-long employment, the gig economy emerged as a new way of doing things. The term, first coined by journalist Tina Brown in 2009, essentially describes variants of contingent work that are transacted via digital means, mostly through so-called digital marketplaces, with each piece of work being akin to an individual "gig" – intended to draw connotations to the working life of a free-spirited musician (Tran & Sokas, 2017).

While "gig economy" is the most widely adopted moniker for this type of digitally intermediated work, a multitude of other terms have also been used, often interchangeably, when referring to this phenomenon. For example, "on-demand economy," "platform economy," and "Uber economy" are all used, particularly by media organisations, while "sharing economy" also features heavily across discourse. However, we urge caution in the interchangeability of terminology as it can often lead to unclear or erroneous conceptualisations of what exactly gig work entails, particularly where subtle yet important distinctions are overlooked (Maselli et al., 2016). In particular, the use of "sharing economy" in place of "gig economy" may be problematic, with the former intended to describe peer-to-peer exchanges to temporarily access underutilised assets, possibly for money, but often without a transparent labour process (De Groen et al., 2016). While such an arrangement is closely related to a particular type of gig work – capital platform work – the presence of a labour-oriented working relationship is typically absent (Duggan et al., 2020).

What makes the gig economy different?

From the perspective of platform organisations, the gig economy represents an innovative, sharp response to the fast-paced nature of the global business environment. Heavily contrasting with the norms and principles of conventional employment, the "gig" business model allows organisations to significantly decrease costs and maintain flexibility in their hiring practices by utilising non-core workers to fill roles traditionally held by salaried employees (Lemmon et al., 2016; Williams et al., 2021). As a result, when compared to conventional employment, the gig economy is not bounded by time: workers are speedily hired, often without regard for their past employment, and with no promise for future employment, legacy pay, or deferred compensation (Friedman, 2014). In this way, gig work creates a new type of hyper-flexibility, where workers remain peripheral to the organisation, and where the risk of economic fluctuations is shifted almost entirely onto individual workers (Harris, 2017).

Importantly, platform organisations who operate in the gig economy identify themselves as technological companies, rather than service providers, by claiming to simply offer a digital infrastructure (i.e. platform or application) that matches supply and demand between workers and requestors (Sundararajan, 2014). Under this business model, all physical assets used in the provision of the service are owned and provided by workers themselves, rather than by the platform organisation. Thus, platform organisations claim that they do not directly provide the services being offered, but rather partner with independent workers who offer their own services to customers via the digital platform. A frequently cited example is that Uber is regarded as the world's largest transportation company (although it is listed as Uber Technologies), yet owns no vehicles. Similarly, Airbnb is larger than the world's top five hotel brands combined, with over 4 million listings worldwide, but has no accommodation properties.

Accordingly, the complex and seemingly intangible foundation upon which the gig economy exists heavily contrasts with the once-standard norms of traditional employment and business operations. In the gig economy, workers are not hired as permanent employees; working conditions need not necessarily provide legal minimum wage levels, nor offer prospects for development or career progression; and platform organisations can operate in a fluid way by functioning on-demand and avoiding the costs of legal employment (Harvey et al., 2017). Instead, gig work is structured around multi-party interactions, where users (both workers and requestors) register on the platform organisation's application to engage with one another under the mediation of the organisation, thereby creating a kind of triadic working relationship (Wood & Lehdonvirta, 2019: Sherman & Morley, 2020). In this way, platform organisations attempt to both maintain, and distance themselves from, responsibility over the markets that they create (Healy et al., 2017).

Today's gig economy

Since its emergence, the gig economy has continued to grow in popularity amongst consumers and has steadily become a more significant part of the labour market, particularly in developed regions (Dupont et al., 2018). While companies that are considered part of the gig economy first started appearing in 2005, with the launch of Amazon Mechanical Turk, these have since spiralled by exhibiting growth in size, number, and revenue (Tran &

Sokas, 2017). In line with this, the gig economy has consistently attracted significant attention – often unwanted, at least from the perspective of platform organisations – from scholars, policymakers, and media organisations across the globe. In most cases, attention has focused on the various employment-based controversies and issues inherent to gig work. This includes debates on the potential erosion of employment standards (Adams et al., 2018); the health and safety of gig workers (Christie & Ward, 2019); the role of algorithmic technologies in managing gig workers (Duggan et al., 2020); job quality (Adamson & Roper, 2019; Myhill et al., 2021), amongst a wide variety of interrelated topics.

Yet, despite increased scrutiny, the gig economy has continued to undergo noteworthy development and expansion, both in terms of organisational incumbents and the range of services on offer (Kaine & Josserand, 2019). In fact, perhaps due to its relatively vague definitional parameters, work in the gig economy currently encompasses a broad range of service offerings, across a vast range of sectors, with the lack of a clearly defined, legal employment relationship often being the only common denominator (Wood et al., 2019). This attempt to redefine the role of labour within platform organisations, wherein the relationship is far more informal, and workers are no longer situated within the boundaries of the firm, continues to challenge legal standards of employment and best-practice organisational policies around the world (Gramano, 2019).

While notoriously difficult to capture accurate data on the size and scale of the gig economy all estimates intimate that numbers employed in this domain are increasing. Gig work continues to grow markedly as a unique subset of contingent work. Roland Berger (2020) suggest that projections typically vary from between 2 and 4 per cent of the working population although it can vary significantly from country to country. For example, Weel et al. (2018) indicate about 0.4 per cent or 34,000 workers are active in gig (platform) work in the Netherlands, while Jeon et al. (2019) indicate a growth of gig workers in Canada from 5.5 per cent in 2005 to 8.2 per cent in 2016. The United States appears similar to Europe, with figures of 0.5 per cent estimated as participating in this form of work as of 2015 (Katz & Krueger, 2016). The United Kingdom appears to have a higher incidence of gig work than Europe and the US, with estimates of over 4 per cent in 2017 (Lepanjuuri et al., 2018), with one in four of these reporting that some form of gig work was their main job (Eurofound, 2017).

However, there is a need for caution in these estimates, given definitional ambiguity. Moreover, measuring the overall size proves difficult because organisations are not obliged to publish figures, and most gig-working arrangements fall outside existing capabilities of labour-market measurement tools. Likewise, many individuals work for more than one platform organisation, patching together a living via multiple gigs, while others perform gig work in additional to holding traditional employment (Tran & Sokas, 2017). Subsequently, although many individual platform organisations boast large worker numbers, relatively little is known regarding how many individuals regularly engage in this work, rather than being one-off or periodic workers (Duggan et al., 2020).

Discourse on gig work

Discourse on gig work traverses from the positive, with emphasis on the innovative business model and apparent benefits for workers, to the negative, with critics viewing the operating model as a means by which businesses lower costs and erode employment standards and labour regulation (Friedman, 2014; Stewart & Stanford, 2017).

The advantages of gig work

Beginning with the more positive reports of gig working, it appears that gig workers, as independent contractors, possess increased autonomy over scheduling through the ability to exert some control over when, where, and how to work (Kuhn & Maleki, 2017). In fact, literature examining such issues highlights that this benefit is likely the key attraction of gig work for individuals as it reinforces the sentiment that the quality and flexibility of work life is greater outside the confines of traditional work settings (Sutherland et al., 2020). Most gig-working arrangements, at least ostensibly, lack hierarchical reporting relationships (Storey et al., 2005), while temporal attachment is relatively low (Kuhn & Maleki, 2017), and thresholds are minimal for crossing between, or working for, multiple platforms (Gherardi & Murgia, 2013). These features also provide organisational benefits through lowering costs substantially given they do not have to provide any of the benefits of traditional employment (De Stefano, 2016).

Consequently, work in the gig economy presents clear advantages for individuals who desire more control over their schedule, who lack full-time roles, or who seek to diversify working opportunities and/or income streams (Kuhn, 2016). Gig work allows participants to work for more than one platform organisation simultaneously, meaning that, at least in theory, there are always alternatives to fall back on if necessary. Thus, with the opportunity to complement or supplement one's income, perhaps in times of crisis or unemployment, it is little surprise that the gig economy thrived and grew from a global financial crisis (Maselli et al., 2016). Evidence also suggests the social side of some gig work roles is seen to be an attractive element for gig workers. For instance, the opportunity to build their social network through meeting other gig workers and through the development of an esprit de corps amongst couriers is considered an enjoyable part of the work (Goods et al., 2019). Ultimately, proponents heavily emphasise the opportunities for those seeking employment, and increased flexibility and autonomy for workers which has seen reference to gig work resembling a type of empowered micro-entrepreneurship (De Stefano, 2016).

The disadvantages of gig work

However, opponents of the gig economy's rapid rise highlight that beyond its promises of independence and flexibility, the gig economy, at its core, represents a stark move towards replacing full-time, benefitted, stable roles with short-term, precarious, and unstable work (Kuhn, 2016). It ultimately is a working arrangement that sees an almost entire lack of any labour protections for gig workers (Frost, 2017). Across most of the scholarly literature, it is these issues – the more troubling and pessimistic viewpoints – that receive the most attention. Gig-working arrangements, by their very nature, are most commonly characterised by low job security, reduced commitment, and decreased loyalty between parties (Wood et al., 2019). Although advocates argue that sacrificing these opportunities is a trade-off for the flexibility afforded to workers, this is challenged by claims that many individuals partaking in gig work seek to develop new skills and networking opportunities useful in furthering their careers (Petriglieri et al., 2019). The seemingly diminished potential for gig workers to gain anything other than extrinsic, monetary rewards in return for their participation raises noteworthy questions about the sustainability and prosperity of these roles in the medium to long term (Kost et al., 2020), along with the extent to which these represent opportunities for quality, meaningful work.

Likewise, the lack of employment status and the overall anonymity of the gig economy renders workers as immediately peripheral to the platform organisation. By utilising algorithmic technologies to manage the working relationship, gig workers are geographically dispersed and typically work in isolation, relying on the organisation's proprietary app for all guidance on processes (Kaine & Josserand, 2019). Consequently, workers have minimal human interaction with management or fellow workers, preventing the development of anything resembling traditional working relationships (Duggan et al., 2020). Moreover, there is a health-and-safety concern to some forms of gig work with several accounts of food delivery drivers being injured or killed while working (e.g. Duffy, 2020; Zhou, 2020).

Major debates in the gig work literature

Literature, commentary, and debate on gig work spans several fields and disciplines. An ongoing surge of research interest in various types of gig work has produced scholarly output with perspectives on people management (Duggan et al., 2020; Meijerink & Keegan, 2019 Meijerink et al., 2021; Shanahan & Smith, 2021), organisational behaviour (Ashford et al., 2018); employment relations (Maffie, 2020); labour law (Blackham, 2018); psychology (Brawley, 2017, Sherman & Morley, 2020); sociology (Vallas & Schor, 2020); and business ethics (Ahsan, 2020), to name a few. We are unable to consider the full and vast range of arguments and issues articulated throughout gig economy scholarship but instead focus upon several broad themes and debates that dominate existing literature. These are briefly outlined in the following subsections, before being expanded upon and developed in greater detail throughout the remainder of this book.

Classification issues

Perhaps the most enduring debate in gig work surrounds the appropriateness of the independent contractor status assigned to workers. Across almost all platform organisations, workers are classified as self-employed independent contractors rather than employees, meaning there exists a highly defined, narrow, and finite set of obligations between the parties (Lemmon et al., 2016). The crux of the issue is that many gig workers report that their working activities are heavily monitored and controlled by the platform organisation, via algorithmic technologies, indicating that these workers are perhaps more akin to being classified as employees rather than independent contractors (Duggan et al., 2020). To further complicate the issue, it has been argued that the nature of the working relationship that exists in the gig economy is so complex and unique that it does not fit easily into the existing definitions of either independent contractor or employee status, and that perhaps a new, hybrid status should be created to encompass those working in the gig economy (Harris & Krueger, 2015).

Yet, despite the complexity of this issue, when roles are advertised by platform organisations, the working arrangement is typically positioned as being mutually beneficial: workers gain the flexibility of choosing when they work, and organisations gain the benefit of nimbleness in expanding or contracting their workforce at will to meet demand without the robust obligations and expenses associated with conventional employment (Lemmon et al., 2016). However, the same characteristics that make gig work attractive also contribute to some of its greatest challenges and pitfalls, as evidenced by the ongoing protests and legal challenges to the independent contractor classification (Schmidt, 2017; Wright et al., 2017).

Likewise, an equally challenging issue exists within the confines of the gig economy itself, where significant uncertainty exists in respect to what gig work does and does not involve. Across literature, there is often little or no distinction between different types of gig work (e.g. work performed remotely versus work performed locally), and in many cases, different forms of contingent labour are commonly subsumed into gig classifications (Howcroft & Bergvall-Kåreborn, 2019; Bernhardt & Thomason, 2017). Given the increasing diversity of platform organisations and services offered, we argue that this is erroneous and that several key differences exist that warrant specific consideration, thereby moving beyond monolithic perspectives to distinguish gig work into three key variants: capital platform work; crowdwork; and app-work (Duggan et al., 2020).

The role of technology and algorithmic management

The defining characteristic of digital platform organisations is that, rather than directly providing the services offered, they instead offer virtual platforms or applications that connect individual workers with requesters (Tran & Sokas, 2017). In other words, these platform organisations state that they are not providers of services (Sundararajan, 2014). While this concept may not seem entirely foreign in today's market, with the gig economy in existence for over a decade, it nevertheless highlights the rapidly changing connectivity, technological disruption, and innovation that enabled the emergence of this business model and work. Such advancements have given consumers unprecedented access to markets, with smartphones quickly becoming sources of incalculable amounts of information, communication, transportation, and employment opportunities (Frost, 2017). The key challenge to emerge from this, particularly from the perspectives of scholars and policymakers, is establishing how best to conceptualise and legislate the gig economy, all while attempting to keep pace with such rapid change.

A by-product of the technological innovation that enabled the gig economy is the use of algorithmic technologies to coordinate, monitor, and manage workers (Wood et al., 2019). These functions, known collectively as algorithmic management, are commonplace in the gig economy, although the specific capabilities and pervasiveness of each function tend to vary between different types of gig work (Rosenblat & Stark, 2016). For the most part, concerns surrounding the role of algorithmic management in gig work are increasingly gaining the attention of HR and employment relations scholars. This is evidenced by a growing body of literature which seeks to examine the various implications arising from the automation of core HR and managerial duties traditionally undertaken by human managers (Duggan et al., 2020; Veen, Barratt & Goods, 2020). Likewise, this issue also aligns with the classification issue within the gig economy, with the rationale that any type of managerial control, even automated, indicates a relationship which more closely resembles employment rather than that of an independent contractor.

Lived experiences of gig workers

The next key theme that we are concerned with within scholarship on gig work relates to the lived experiences of gig workers. Given the extensive nature of the classification and technology-related issues outlined previously, and the implications these hold for individuals engaged in this work, it is crucially important to understand how gig workers navigate the complexity and precarity inherent to their roles. Although the employment status of gig workers is made clear from the outset, many roles in the gig economy require an element of social connection via the provision of services to requestors. Thus, it seems logical that topics such as motivation, satisfaction, and well-being warrant consideration in this context (Kuhn, 2016).

While one may argue that much gig work is often low-skill and the working conditions are not wholly different to similar roles wherein digital intermediation is not a factor (e.g. food delivery, transportation), it is important to acknowledge that the role of digital platforms in gig work represents an evolution in and increased visibility of contingent work (Tran & Sokas, 2017). In particular, the gig economy has engaged many workers who are highly educated and previously held roles in traditional employment settings, perhaps due to sudden unemployment or the prospect of supplemental or diversified income streams (Kuhn & Maleki, 2017), or being taken with the promise of full autonomy on when to work. In such cases, it is argued that the gig economy increases the vulnerability of these workers to job insecurity, lack of occupational health protections, and potential independent contractor misclassification (Tran & Sokas, 2017). Gig workers are extremely scalable, being provided "just-in-time" and compensated on a "pay-as-you-go" basis, thereby granting a level of flexibility and disposability previously unheard of for workers and organisations (De Stefano, 2016).

The plethora of issues to be explored, simply from the perspective of the gig worker alone, emphasises the stark and wide-ranging risks faced by individuals engaged in this relatively novel form of labour. Sometimes described as a new cohort of "invisible workers" (De Stefano, 2016), it quickly becomes apparent that in-depth understanding of how gig workers experience and perceive the challenges associated with their roles has not been subject to sufficient empirical scrutiny across the literature (Wu et al., 2019).

Rapidly developing research area

Finally, a broader issue across gig economy scholarship is that there still exists a notable lack of large-scale empirical studies which examine many of the issues outlined above. Within academia, the concept of the gig economy is still relatively novel (Kuhn, 2016). Likewise, as highlighted throughout this chapter, significant complexities exist in attempting to effectively define and conceptualise gig work, and in seeking to understand the experiences of individuals engaged in roles, which may also contribute to the lack of empirical studies (Bergman & Jean, 2016).

That being said, research on gig work is currently experiencing a significant surge in popularity, with conceptual, provocative, qualitative studies, and special issues becoming increasingly common. Some quantitative studies also exist, often studying singular platform organisations. However, these remain relatively scarce, perhaps due to the difficulty in accessing and capturing the experiences of a geographically dispersed and often invisible workforce (Maselli et al., 2016). This is an important point to highlight as accessing the gig worker population is not a straightforward matter given that it falls outside normal organisational boundaries.

Book structure

The structure of this book is as follows. Chapter 2 examines the varying definitions and variants of gig work that are featured in extant literature. In doing so, this chapter delineates three different types and forms of gig work, highlighting the need to adopt parameters around how and why work may be classified as being part of the gig economy. For the purpose of gaining a more intricate understanding of this relatively novel type of labour, the chapter seeks to move the debate away from a monolithic perspective by distinguishing gig work into three typologies, namely capital platform work, crowdwork, and app-work. This chapter will also identify that the common denominator across forms of gig work, and a critical distinguishing feature to contingent labour, is the presence of an intermediary in the form of the digital platform organisation.

Chapter 3 focuses on the central role of technology and, more particularly, algorithms in the gig economy. Algorithms embedded within digital platform organisations, by autonomously making decisions based on models or rules without explicit human intervention (Eurofound, 2018), appear to govern the rules used to select and manage labour through managing supply and demand in the market, while also mediating and closely monitoring the work performed (Gandini, 2019). Algorithms also can track the movements of some gig workers, predict periods of high demand, and assign work. In this chapter, we highlight the current state of knowledge on algorithmic management and discuss how this novel workforce management tool appears to be increasingly implemented in the gig economy as a means of removing or replacing typical HR processes such as recruitment and performance management.

In Chapter 4, the implications of gig work for individual workers are considered. For example, we examine the lived experiences of gig workers in navigating a heavily digitalised, multi-party working relationship. In doing so, this chapter explores issues such as the fragmented nature of employment relations, the constrained ability of gig workers to exercise significant autonomy in their roles, and career development-related issues for individuals engaged in this work on a full-time or long-term basis.

Finally, Chapter 5 considers the future of gig work. In this chapter, we synthesise the most critical points covered in the preceding chapters to propose a future research agenda around key themes. Additionally, we move beyond the specific areas examined throughout chapters to consider several important areas that have remained unexplored, underdeveloped, or peripheral in research on gig work to date.

Conclusion

This opening chapter has provided a concise overview of the emergence and growth of the gig economy as a field of scholarly interest. Throughout the past decade, the gig economy has become increasingly recognised as a disruptive by-product of technological change and the increasing precarity of work and employment (Barley et al., 2017). Even sporadic engagement with the surge of scholarly research on gig work illustrates the continuous developments, ongoing controversies, and unresolved debates that dominate discourse in this domain. Likewise, there is little evidence to suggest that the rapid pace at which the gig economy emerged and developed will subside as we move further into the 21st century, with literature and policy often struggling to keep pace as new types of platform organisations and enhanced algorithmic technologies continue to be unveiled, implemented, and understood. However, before delving into the more prominent and pervasive issues and controversies in this domain, it is crucially important that readers first develop a strong foundational understanding of what exactly the gig economy is (and is not), when and why it emerged, and how gig work is characterised across existing scholarship. As outlined throughout this chapter, this knowledge is instrumental in effectively identifying and fully understanding the diverse range of challenges and opportunities represented by work in the gig economy.

With that in mind, what is the current state of research on gig work? And how far has scholarship developed in terms of addressing these opportunities and challenges? The following chapters have been carefully crafted to help address these questions. Gig work challenges many aspects of our understanding of employment, management practices, careers, and several related fields. With the continued expansion of the gig economy across sectors and regions, scholars, policymakers, governments, and organisations have come under increasing pressure to develop or adapt frameworks that appropriately encapsulate the nuances and complexities of gig work. Achieving this responsiveness is increasingly important in the quest to better understand how this new economy is influencing and impacting upon the livelihoods of workers (Graham et al., 2017), along with the wider societal implications.

Note

1 Funding Acknowledgement: This research is funded by the Irish Research Council through the Government of Ireland Postgraduate Scholarship Programme [GOIPG/2018/2196].

References

Adams, A., Freedman, J., & Prassl, J. (2018). Rethinking legal taxonomies for the gig economy. *Oxford Review of Economic Policy*, 34 (3): 475–494.

Adamson, M., & Roper, I. (2019). "Good" jobs and "bad" jobs: Contemplating job quality in different contexts. *Work, Employment and Society*, 33 (4): 551–559.

Ahsan, M. (2020). Entrepreneurship and ethics in the sharing economy: A critical perspective. *Journal of Business Ethics*, 161: 19–33.

Ashford, S.J., Caza, B.B., & Reid, E.M. (2018). From surviving to thriving in the gig economy: A research agenda for individuals in the new world of work. *Research in Organizational Behavior*, 38: 23–41.

Barley, S.R., Bechky, B.A., & Milliken, F.J. (2017). The changing nature of work: Careers, identities, and work lives in the 21st century. *Academy of Management Discoveries*, 3 (2): 111–115.

Bergman, M.E., & Jean, V.A. (2016). Where have all the "workers" gone? A critical analysis of the unrepresentativeness of our samples relative to the labour market in the industrial-organisational psychology literature. *Industrial and Organisational Psychology*, 9 (1): 84–113.

Bernhardt, A., & Thomason, S. (2017). What do we know about gig work in California? An analysis of independent contracting. *UC Berkeley Labour Centre,* 1–23.

Blackham, A. (2018). "We are all entrepreneurs now": Options and new approaches for adapting equality law for the gig economy. *International Journal of Comparative Labour Law and Industrial Relations,* 34 (4): 413–434.

Brawley, A.M. (2017). The big, gig picture: We can't assume the same constructs matter. *Industrial and Organisational Psychology,* 10 (4): 687–696.

Cennamo, C. (2019). Competing in digital markets: A platform-based perspective. *Academy of Management Perspectives.*

Christie, N., & Ward, H. (2019). The health and safety risks for people who drive for work in the gig economy. *Journal of Transport & Health,* 13: 115–127.

De Groen, W.P., Maselli, I., & Fabo, B. (2016). The digital market for local services: A one-night stand for workers? An example from the on-demand economy. *Centre of European Policy Studies,* 133: 1–28.

De Stefano, V. (2016). The rise of the "just-in-time" workforce: On-demand work, crowdwork and labour protection in the gig economy. *International Labour Office: Conditions of Work and Employment Series,* 71: 1–35.

Duffy, R. (2020). Delivery cyclist dies in hospital following Dublin hit-and-run. https://www.thejournal.ie/dublin-hit-and-run-3-5193331-Sep2020/ [Accessed 21 January 2021].

Duggan, J., Sherman, U., Carbery, R., & McDonnell, A. (2020). Algorithmic management and app-work in the gig economy: A research agenda for employment relations and HRM. *Human Resource Management Journal,* 30 (1): 114–132.

Dupont, J., Hughes, S., Wolf, R., & Wride, S. (2018). *Freedom and Flexibility: The Relationship Deliveroo Riders Have With the Labour Market.* Public First, London.

Eurofound (2017). *Non-standard Forms of Employment: Recent Trends and Future Prospects.* Eurofound, Dublin.

Eurofound (2018). *Automation, Digitalisation and Platforms: Implications for Work and Employment,* Publications Office of the European Union, Luxembourg.

Friedman, G. (2014). Workers without employers: Shadow corporations and the rise of the gig economy. *Review of Keynesian Economics,* 2 (2): 171–188.

Frost, J. (2017). Uber and the gig economy: Can the legal world keep up? *American Bar Association: The SciTech Lawyer,* 13 (2): 4–7.

Gandini, A. (2019). Labour process theory and the gig economy. *Human Relations,* 72 (6): 1039–1056.

Gherardi, S., & Murgia, A. (2013). By hook or by crook: Flexible workers between exploration and exploitation. In M. Holmqvist & A. Spicer (Eds.), *Research in the Sociology of Organizations,* 75–103. Emerald, York.

Goods, C., Veen, A., & Barratt, T., 2019. "Is your gig any good?" Analysing job quality in the Australian platform-based food-delivery sector. *Journal of Industrial Relations,* 61 (4): 502–527.

Graham, M., Hjorth, I., & Lehdonvirta, V. (2017). Digital labour and development: Impacts of global digital labour platforms and the gig economy on worker livelihoods. *Transfer: European Review of Labour and Research*, 23 (2): 135–162.

Gramano, E. (2019). Digitalisation and work: Challenges from the platform economy. *Journal of the Academy of Social Sciences*, 15 (4): 476–488.

Harris, B. (2017). Uber, lyft, and regulating the sharing economy. *Seattle University Law Review*, 41 (1): 269–285.

Harris, S.D., & Krueger, A.B. (2015). *A Proposal for Modernising Labour Laws for Twenty-First-Century Work: The "Independent Worker."* The Hamilton Project, Discussion Paper 2015/10.

Harvey, G., Rhodes, C., Vachhani, S.J., & Williams, K. (2017). Neo-villeiny and the service sector: The case of hyper flexible and precarious work in fitness centres. *Work, Employment and Society*, 31 (1): 19–35.

Healy, J., Nicholson, D., & Pekarek, A. (2017). Should we take the gig economy seriously? *Labour and Industry: A Journal of the Social and Economic Relations of Work*, 27 (3): 232–248.

Howcroft, D., & Bergvall-Kåreborn, B. (2019). A typology of crowdwork platforms. *Work, Employment and Society*, 33 (1): 21–38.

Huws, U., & Joyce, S. (2016). Size of the UK's "gig economy" revealed for the first time. *Crowd Working Survey, Foundation for European Progressive Studies*, 1–4.

Jabagi, N., Croteau, A.M., Audebrand, L.K., & Marsan, J. (2019). Gig workers' motivation: Thinking beyond carrots and sticks. *Journal of Managerial Psychology*, 34 (4): 192–213.

Jeon, S.H., Liu, H., & Ostrovsky, Y. (2019). *Measuring the Gig Economy in Canada Using Administrative Data*. Analytical Studies Branch Research Paper Series, 11F0019M No. 437.

Kaine, S., & Josserand, E. (2019). The organisation and experience of work in the gig economy. *Journal of Industrial Relations*, 61 (4): 479–501.

Katz, L.F., & Krueger, A.B. (2019). The rise and nature of alternative work arrangements in the United States, 1995-2015. *ILR Review*, 72 (2): 382–416.

Kost, D., Fieseler, C., & Wong, S.I. (2020). Boundaryless careers in the gig economy: An oxymoron? *Human Resource Management Journal*, 30 (1): 100–113.

Kuhn, K.M. (2016). The rise of the gig economy and implications for understanding work and workers. *Industrial and Organisational Psychology*, 9 (1): 157–162.

Kuhn, K.M., & Maleki, A. (2017). Micro-entrepreneurs, dependent contractors, and instaserfs: Understanding online labour platform workforces. *Academy of Management Perspectives*, 31 (3): 183–200.

Lemmon, G., Wilson, M.S., Posig, M., & Glibkowski, B.C. (2016). Psychological contract development, distributive justice, and performance of independent contractors: The role of negotiation behaviours and the fulfilment of resources. *Journal of Leadership and Organisational Studies*, 23 (4): 424–439.

Lepanjuuri, K., Wishart, R., & Cornick, P. (2018). *The Characteristics of Those in the Gig Economy*. Department for Business, Energy & Industrial Strategy. London, UK.

18   *Work in the gig economy*

Maffie, M.D. (2020). The role of digital communities in organising gig workers. *Industrial Relations: A Journal of Economy and Society*, 59 (1): 123–149.

Manyika, J., Lund, S., Bughin, J., Robinson, K., Mischke, J., & Mahajan, D. (2016). *Independent Work, Choice, Necessity and the Gig Economy*. McKinsey Global Institute.

Maselli, I., Lenaerts, K., & Beblavy, M. (2016). Five things we need to know about the on-demand economy. *Centre for European Policy Studies*, 21: 1–10.

McGaughey, E. (2018). Taylorooism: When network technology meets corporate power. *Industrial Relations Journal*, 49 (5–6): 459–472.

Meijerink, J., & Keegan, A. (2019). Conceptualizing human resource management in the gig economy: Toward a platform ecosystem perspective. *Journal of Managerial Psychology*, 34 (4): 214–232.

Meijerink, J., Keegan, A., & Bondarouk, T. (2021). Having their cake and eating it too? Online labor platforms and human resource management as a case of institutional complexity. *International Journal of Human Resource Management*, doi:10.1080/09585192.2020.1867616

Myhill, K., Richards, J., & Sang, K. (2021). Job quality, fair work and gig work: The lived experience of gig workers. *The International Journal of Human Resource Management*, doi:10.1080/09585192.2020.1867612

Norlander,P., Jukic, N., Varma, A., & Nestorov, S. (2021). The effects of technological supervision on gig workers: Organizational control and motivation of Uber, taxi, and limousine drivers, *The International Journal of Human Resource Management*, doi:10.1080/09585192.2020.1867614

Petriglieri, G., Ashford, S.J., & Wrzesniewski, A. (2019). Agony and ecstasy in the gig economy: Cultivating holding environments for precarious and personalised work identities. *Administrative Science Quarterly*, 64 (1): 124–170.

Roland Berger (2020). The future of the gig economy. https://www.rolandberger.com/en/Insights/Publications/The-future-of-the-gig-economy.html [Accessed 18 January 2021].

Rosenblat, A., & Stark, L. (2016). Algorithmic labour and information asymmetries: A case study of Uber's drivers. *International Journal of Communications*, 10 (27): 3758–3784.

Schmidt, F.A. (2017). *Digital Labour Markets in the Platform Economy: Mapping the Political Challenges of Crowd Work and Gig Work*. Friedrich-Ebert-Stiftung, Berlin, Germany.

Shanahan, G., & Smith, M. (2021). Fair's fair: Psychological contracts and power in platform work. *The International Journal of Human Resource Management*, doi :10.1080/09585192.2020.1867615

Shapiro, A. (2017). Between autonomy and control: Strategies of arbitrage in the on-demand economy. *New Media & Society*, 20 (8): 2954–2971.

Sherman, U.P., & Morley, M.J. (2020). What do we measure and how do we elicit it? The case for the use of repertory grid technique in multi-party psychological contract research. *European Journal of Work and Organizational Psychology*, 29 (2): 230–242.

Smith, R., & Leberstein, S. (2015). *Rights on Demand: Ensuring Workplace Standards and Worker Security in the On-Demand Economy*. National Employment Law Project, New York.

Stewart, A., & Stanford, J. (2017). Regulating work in the gig economy: What are the options? *The Economic and Labour Relations Review*, 28 (3): 420–437.

Storey, J., Salaman, G., & Platman, K. (2005). Living with enterprise in an enterprise economy: Freelance and contract workers in the media. *Human Relations*, 58 (8): 1033–1054.

Sundararajan, A. (2014). What Airbnb gets about culture that Uber doesn't. *Harvard Business Review*, 27 November.

Sutherland, W., Jarrahi, M.H., Dunn, M., & Nelson, S.B. (2020). Work precarity and gig literacies in online freelancing. *Work, Employment and Society*, 34 (3): 457–475.

Tran, M., & Sokas, R.K. (2017). The gig economy and contingent work: An occupational health assessment. *Journal of Occupational and Environmental Medicine*, 59 (4): 63–66.

Vallas, S., & Schor, J.B. (2020). What do platforms do? Understanding the gig economy. *Annual Review of Sociology*, 46: 273–294.

Veen, A., Barratt, T., & Goods, C. (2020). Platform-capital's app-etite for control: A labour process analysis of food-delivery work in Australia. *Work, Employment and Society*, 34 (3): 388–406.

Weel, B., van der Werff, S., Bennaars, H., Scholte, R., Fijnje, J., Westerveld, M., Mertens, T. (2018). *De Opkomst en Groei van de Kluseconomie in Nederland*. SEO (SEO Economisch Onderzoek), Amsterdam.

Weil, D. (2017). How to make employment fair in an age of contracting and temp work. *Harvard Business Review*, 24 March.

Williams, P., McDonald, P., & Mayes, R. (2021). Recruitment in the gig economy: Attraction and selection on digital platforms, *International Journal of Human Resource Management*, doi:10.1080/09585192.2020.1867613

Wood, A.J., & Lehdonvirta, V. (2019). *Platform Labour and Structured Antagonism: Understanding the Origins of Protest in the Gig Economy*. Paper presented at the Oxford Internet Institute Platform Economy Seminar Series, 5 March.

Wood, A.J., Graham, M., Lehdonvirta, V., & Hjorth, I. (2019). Good gig, bad gig: Autonomy and algorithmic control in the global gig economy. *Work, Employment and Society*, 33 (1): 56–75.

Wright, C.F., Wailes, N., Bamber, G.J., & Lansbury, R.D. (2017). Beyond national systems, towards a gig economy? A research agenda for international and comparative employment relations. *Employee Responsibilities and Rights Journal*, 29 (4): 247–257.

Wu, Q., Zhang, H., Li, Z., & Liu, K. (2019). Labor control in the gig economy: Evidence from Uber in China. *Journal of Industrial Relations*, 61 (4): 574–596.

Zhou, N. (2020). NSW government announced taskforce to investigate food delivery deaths. *The Guardian*. https://www.theguardian.com/australia-news /2020/nov/24/food-delivery-driver-killed-in-sydney-is-the-fifth-death-in-two-m onths [Accessed 21 January 2021].

2 Classifying gig work

Introduction

Research on the gig economy, despite being in its relative infancy, has produced a multitude of conceptualisations of working arrangements in this field of inquiry. Perhaps as a result of differing perspectives on what precisely the gig economy entails, the range of conceptualisations complicates the broader stream of discourse on gig work by setting unclear definitional parameters and conflating various classifications and variants (Bernhardt & Thomason, 2017; Duggan et al., 2020). As a result, it has been difficult for scholars, policymakers, and legislators alike to effectively address the issues inherent to "gig work" as a whole – because, put simply, much of the literature has struggled to identify what exactly gig work encompasses.

An important starting point, therefore, in considering the challenges and opportunities of gig work is to focus on explicitly identifying the distinctive features of this form of labour, especially in contrast to established and more extensively studied forms of contingent work – many of which share noteworthy similarities with gig work. However, simply identifying these distinctive features does not go far enough. Consequently, "gig work" – as an encompassing umbrella-type term – requires a greater depth of analysis in recognition that there is not just one type of gig work.

In this chapter, we synthesise the extant literature to provide greater clarity and help address both issues. First, we examine the increasing growth of contingent working arrangements and the disruptive role of gig work in this sphere. We place a particular emphasis on differentiating gig work as a distinctive, novel form of contingent work. Second, drawing from Duggan et al. (2020), the chapter moves away from problematic aggregations to set out different types of gig work. This sees us delineate three key variants of gig work: app-work; crowdwork; and capital platform work. Finally, we outline the specific nature of the working relationships that likely exist in

DOI: 10.4324/9780429351488-2

each of these variants, while also highlighting several broader implications for the world of work.

Key chapter takeaways

- Gig work possesses several distinctive features that differentiate this form of labour from other non-traditional types of work.
- The role of technology, and particularly the role of platform organisations as digital intermediaries, is a principal distinguishing feature of gig work.
- There are three key variants of gig work: app-work; crowdwork; and capital platform work.
- Within management scholarship, the app-work variant and its accompanying working arrangement is especially disruptive to traditional conceptualisations of an employment relationship.

The changing nature of work

As one of the most basic building blocks of economic activity, it is not unreasonable to assert that work, or the experience of work, shapes or defines individuals (Bryson, 2018). In this way, while recognising work as a cornerstone vehicle for taxation that contributes to wider societal welfare, it is also important to consider the influence of working experiences – either good or bad – on the well-being of individuals. While this strand of research has consistently drawn interest, it has often done so in conjunction with the well-established norms of conventional work and employment. In other words: where the working relationship is characterised by a level of commitment; where wages and benefits increase over time; and where development opportunities arise by allowing committed and high-performing employees to "climb the ladder" (Weil, 2017).

There has also been recognition that work and working arrangements are not static but fluctuate over time. There are many enablers of such changes with key macro factors including the substantial shift from dominant, national, manufacturing economies to more global, technological, and services-focused markets. Moreover, there have been major demographic shifts which further impact on the nature of employment practice (Kalleberg, 2000). Reflecting early conceptualisations by Wolfe (1941), legal and organisational scholars have consistently attempted to keep pace with such changes. Although the success of scholarship in achieving this objective has perhaps varied over past decades, there are generally agreed-upon characteristics or features that have tended to accompany conceptualisations of "work." For example, most point to the idea of an employee being "controlled" by the organisation, "in the service" of an "employer," "directing" the work process in exchange for "remuneration," or the reciprocal obligations involved (Cappelli & Keller, 2013; Connelly & Gallagher, 2004; Schein, 1980).

Work is increasingly occurring in organisations "with a more permeable boundary, where work – and people – move inside and outside more freely" (Boudreau et al., 2015). In effect, employment models have been moving from inward and organisationally focused to a more open system characterised by a more external market orientation (Bidwell et al., 2013). As a result, the ways that workers engage with organisations, and vice versa, is undergoing considerable change. Most significant has been the shift away from the once-standard employment model, characterised by full-time, permanent contracts, towards temporary, short-term, part-time, and informal arrangements (Harvey et al., 2017).

It is both expected and understandable that the norms and characteristics of "employment" also change significantly when the individuals operating in roles are not legally classified as employees. Thus, for temporary workers, independent contractors, day labourers, and so on, most of the benefits and protections that accompany conventional employment are either significantly reduced or entirely eradicated. For instance, wage growth is typically stunted, opportunities for on-the-job training and development are diminished, pathways to upward advancement are unavailable, and access to the likes of unemployment insurance and workers' compensation are withheld (Weil, 2017). In today's workplace, we recognise the increasing presence of these precarious working arrangements, where the ad hoc terms and conditions outlined above are more commonplace (Bonet et al., 2013; Harvey et al., 2017).

The rise of contingent working arrangements

Different patterns of working habits, greater variety of forms of employment contracts, and increased pressure for flexibility on both employers and employees have fundamentally transformed contemporary working arrangements (Guest, 2004). Such trends have increased in growth and profile since the 1970s, solidifying concerns that the overall quality of employment is subject to increased risk and precarity (Cochrane & McKeown, 2015). A significant consequence of these developments is the emergence of "contingent work" as a ubiquitous term and a core dimension of the business landscape. Typically referring to workers that do not have an implicit or explicit understanding that the employment will be continuous, contingent work is a general term for forms of employment tied to the completion of a specific task for a relatively short duration (Kroon & Paauwe, 2013; McLean Parks et al., 1998). Indeed, a variety of contemporary employment relationships fall into the category of contingent work (Barley et al., 2017).

Contingent work originally referred to a conditional employment relationship initiated by an immediate need for labour, perhaps due to increased demand, but quickly expanded to include virtually any work arrangement that might differ from the commonly perceived norm of a full-time wage (Felstead & Jewson, 1999; Rosenberg & Lapidus, 1999). As firms move away from traditional, full-time employment, flexible labour is conveniently thought of as part-time, temporary, and self-employed. However, with continuous growth in this area, particularly since the 1990s, it is now increasingly seen to include a host of other types of work, such as freelancing, subcontracting, zero-hours contracts, seasonal working, flexitime, and consultancy work (Ashford et al., 2007). While all these arrangements differ, sometimes in minor ways, a universal feature is their divergence from the "norm" of standard, full-time employment which is based on a formal contract and legally binding terms and conditions (Felstead & Jewson, 1999; Helfen, 2015).

Traditionally, contingent work was more closely concentrated in clerical, low-skill, and low-wage industrial occupations (Finegold et al., 2005; Kalleberg, 2012). Yet, the pace of change in the modern economy, particularly in technology and the development of new business models, has expanded our understanding of what constitutes contingent work to the degree that employment opportunities in this domain now often require highly skilled workers in exchange for high remuneration (Fisher & Connelly, 2017; Taylor et al., 2017). For some scholars, this broadened perspective has led to contingent work emerging as the new "normal" type of contemporary employment (Inkson et al., 2012; Connelly & Gallagher, 2004). Because contingent work exists on a broad continuum, we urge caution in attempting to estimate the exact size of this segment of the labour market. However, we may draw some insights on the scope of this growth from estimates that such work arrangements affect 75 per cent of the global workforce, with some large companies using contingent workers to form up to 30 per cent of their workforce (Geller & Mazor, 2011; Harvey et al., 2017).

The argument for contingent work

Several reasons underpin the substantial growth in contingent work. The most obvious rationale positions contingent work as a response to the nature of the fast-paced, global business environment in which organisations operate, wherein there has been a notable shift in how organisations manage their human resources (Lemmon et al., 2016). Essentially, in this climate, the notion of full-time employment, with all the associated legal requirements and expenses, seems irreconcilable with organisations' needs for competitiveness. Yet, this perspective often fails to recognise that organisations' needs for such flexible arrangements may also be irreconcilable with the needs of workers, who, under these arrangements, find themselves excluded from the "official" workforce (Fynes et al., 1996).

Of course, in many cases, the use of contingent working arrangements is simply to address specific, short-term labour-force needs, such as busy seasonal periods or to replace a temporarily absent worker. Nevertheless, there is also a growing number of organisations that are coming to rely intensively on such arrangements and have made them the mainstay of their operations (International Labour Office, 2016). The fetish for short-term financial results and the power of the shareholder significantly impacts organisational decision-making and appears to be the reason for the rise of such "workforce-on-demand" models (Dundon & Rafftery, 2018; Spreitzer et al., 2017). The heavy economic financialization approach that is now so pervasive brings increased pressure for flexibility and to reduce the provision of secure jobs and associated (costly) benefits.

Flexible staffing arrangements, for the most part, present significant benefits for employers. When compared to regular, full-time workers, non-standard arrangements reduce labour costs ranging from minimum wage entitlements to a variety of benefits (Rosenberg & Lapidus, 1999). Such intense flexibility allows organisations to call upon workers at short notice to help meet demand, to address fluctuations in labour supply, or to fulfil the need for specialist skills not available in-house (Lambert, 2008). Likewise, from a public policy perspective, employment legislation has, broadly speaking, focused on protecting workers in traditional employment relationships, and has subsequently struggled to maintain pace with the evolution and continued growth of contingent work (Cappelli et al., 1997). Thus, these legislative gaps have also worked in the favour of organisations seeking to utilise a contingent workforce.

For workers, the argument for contingent work is less clear, with literature highlighting a range of advantages and disadvantages. When considering the experiences of contingent workers, important considerations include whether participation is voluntary, the length of time spent in these roles, and the extent to which such arrangements can enhance the workers' employability rather than increase their insecurity (Ghosh et al., 2009). With these issues in mind, opportunities for workers include entry or re-entry to the labour market, networking opportunities, and of course, the flexibility afforded by such arrangements (Felstead & Jewson, 1999).

Without the constraints of traditional hierarchical arrangements, contingent workers are free – in theory, at least – to exercise discretion over their working time and career management (Donnelly, 2008). On the other hand, contingent work is typically associated with greater insecurity and lower pay than permanent roles. Subsequently, individuals must often work longer hours with increased work intensity and perhaps hold multiple roles, resulting in longer overall hours and irregular, unpredictable work schedules and income streams (Wood, 2016). Thus, the extent to which individuals freely choose contingent work as their preferred approach is difficult to ascertain. There appears to be a desire amongst workers for greater flexibility and autonomy in how and when they work but the reality, especially in the rise of hyper-flexible working arrangements, may be quite different in practice (Wood et al., 2019).

Contingent work: where does the gig economy fit in?

Although literature has conceptualised work and workers in different ways, how platform organisations in the gig economy view their workers is especially controversial and represents a departure from existing understandings. In distancing themselves from legal responsibility towards "employees," most platform organisations have adopted other monikers for worker classification (e.g. "turkers" with crowdsourcing platform Amazon Mechanical Turk; "taskers" with handyman platform TaskRabbit; "riders" with food-delivery platform Deliveroo). Beneath these monikers, most gig workers are classified as self-employed independent contractors. For example, rideshare platform organisation Uber has almost four million driver partners across 700+ cities worldwide (Madrigal, 2019), but only legally employs approximately 22,000 in total (Uber, 2019). Similarly, Lyft, another ride-hailing service, operates in 600+ locations across the US and Canada with almost two million drivers on the platform, but employs less than 5,000 (McNeill, 2019). Likewise, Deliveroo has almost 40,000 "riders" in 200 cities but only directly employs an estimated 2,000 (Hurley, 2018).

Like many contingent workers, those operating in the gig economy are "hired" on a job-by-job basis and are not afforded the employment rights and benefits allotted to core workers (Lemmon et al., 2016). As such, the gig economy effectively represents hyper-individualism with most transactional costs and associated risk passed to labour (Dundon & Rafftery, 2018). Due to this, gig workers form a relatively cheap form of labour for platform organisations: workers are only paid for tasks completed and the exact time spent working; minimal training is provided by the platform organisation; and workers must supply their own "set of tools" to complete tasks (Duggan et al., 2020; Friedman, 2014). For firms, estimates indicate that engaging the services of independent contractors costs 20 to 30 per cent less than employees, clearly illustrating the appeal of this scenario for platform organisations (Etzioni, 2018). There are, however, several cases being taken by gig workers, many with the support of independent unions, challenging the legal status of their employment. Most of these claims are based around the intense levels of surveillance and control implemented by platform organisations which it is argued do not readily align with the specific legal requirements of the independent contractor status (McGaughey, 2018). In almost all cases, gig workers are integral to the core business of the platform organisation, and as a result, they seemingly are not granted full control over aspects of the methods and means of their work in the way that regular independent contractors may be (Harris & Krueger, 2015).

With this key distinction in mind, it is important to recognise that the working arrangements found in the gig economy represent a new form of contingent labour. As explained, gig work should not be mistakenly subsumed or conflated with existing forms of non-standard employment (Duggan et al., 2020). Instead, when situating gig work in the literature on employment classifications, it is most appropriately viewed as a hybrid of contingent work types (Kuhn, 2016).

Figure 2.1 illustrates how gig work compares to other types of employment, both conventional and contingent. For example, gig work has obvious similarities to independent contracting (Carr et al., 2017) and forms of subcontracting with the involvement of at least three parties (i.e. the platform organisation, gig worker, and customer/requester). Gig work also bears similarities to temporary employment, which is neither full-time nor open-ended (Friedman, 2014); temporary agency work, which distributes work via third-party labour intermediaries (Ward et al., 2001); and zero-hour contracts, where no guaranteed hours are offered (O'Sullivan et al., 2015). The precarity of these arrangements makes them comparable to aspects of gig work in terms of a lack of commitment to long-term relationships, flexible working hours, project-based work, and piece-rate payments.

The role of the digital platform organisation

The critical distinguishing feature of gig work when compared to other contingent labour is the presence of a digital intermediary in the form of the platform organisation. Platform organisations represent a new way of organising work and offering services, functioning as online businesses that facilitate commercial interactions between at least two parties – workers and customers (Gramano, 2019). These organisations are having profound impacts even in some of the most highly regulated industries. For example,

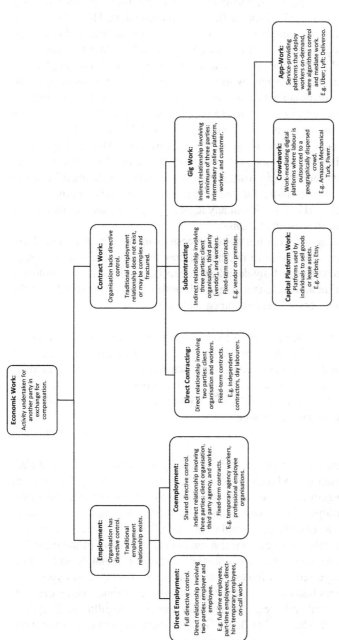

Figure 2.1 Situating gig work in the sphere of working arrangements, cited from Duggan et al. (2020) and adapted from Cappelli and Keller (2013)

the taxi industry and its (employed) drivers are subject to a plethora of insurance requirements, administrative, social, and tax responsibilities, yet the likes of Uber and Lyft appear free of such constraints. These digital platform organisations enable the meeting between the worker and customer, and, in doing so, mediate this relationship (Gandini, 2019). Likewise, it is the digital on-demand, or work-as-required, principle found in platform organisations that sees gig workers, as subordinate personnel, become increasingly disposable (Todolí-Signes, 2017). This can lead to siphoning traditional jobs into a more insecure labour market with inferior terms and conditions. Such organisations appear bereft of the need to be compliant with many long-standing regulatory provisions. Moving beyond the traditional bilateral relations between worker and employer, the trilateral arrangements found in gig work instead allow the platform organisation to create value by facilitating the interaction between at least two other parties (Collier et al., 2017) but without any legal responsibility as they merely act as a mediator in such an exchange.

Literature on gig work has placed intense focus and scrutiny on platform organisations, attempting to understand how they operate, and more specifically, attempting to fully decipher the precise nature of the technologies used to monitor and manage workers. It is unsurprising, then, that the resulting perceptions often starkly contrast with one another:

> Platforms are seen as entrepreneurial incubators, digital cages, accelerants of precarity, and chameleons adapting to their environments. Each of these devices has limitations, which leads us to introduce an alternative image of platforms: as permissive potentates that externalise responsibility and control over economic transactions while still exercising concentrated power.
>
> (Vallas & Schor, 2020: 273)

While research is perhaps still seeking to fully realise the intricacies of platform organisations and their capabilities, a more widely recognised truth is that these organisations serve to reconfigure the nature of work and working relationships. This reconfiguration is achieved, for example, by rendering workers as entirely peripheral to the organisation to the extent that gig workers are unlikely to ever meet a human representative of the organisation; by using algorithmic technologies to monitor, manage, and control large and dispersed workforces; and by creating a new type of hyper-flexibility wherein tasks only exist for a short period of time, with extremely low commitment and great insecurity for workers (Birgillito & Birgillito, 2018; Kuhn & Maleki, 2017). Yet, despite mounting criticism over these and related conditions, platform organisations argue that efforts to change or regulate the gig economy will crush the technological and labour innovation that they have advanced (Smith & Leberstein, 2015). Such debates are likely to continue for some time.

While a level of uncertainty may exist in respect to what gig work does and does not involve, and despite gig work bearing outward similarities to several other types of contingent and non-standard work, key differences also exist (Bernhardt & Thomason, 2017; Howcroft & Bergvall-Kåreborn, 2019). These distinguishing features, mostly relating to the pervasive role of technology in gig work (Kuhn, 2016), warrant specific consideration in recognising that gig work should not be subsumed into various forms of contingent labour, but instead classified as a novel work form.

Towards distinguishing the variants of gig work

Having established that gig work represents a different type of contingent labour, the next necessary step in developing our understanding is recognising that there is not just one variant of gig work, nor is there a universal set of "rules" to be implemented when discussing work in this sphere. For example, we argue that individuals who occasionally boost their income by renting out apartments or spare bedrooms on Airbnb, an online platform for property rental, are very different from those who make a living by working for ride-hailing or food-delivery services like Uber or Deliveroo (Cheng & Foley, 2019; Rozzi, 2018). Likewise, we contend that these are strikingly different from crowdworking platforms, such as Amazon Mechanical Turk, which connect businesses with freelance workers of varying levels of skillsets (Berg, 2016). Because work and conditions are hugely individualised across platform organisations, it is worthwhile to differentiate between gig work variants to effectively identify and address the implications related to people management, employment relations, and worker classification.

By identifying the similarities and differences across types of gig work, Duggan et al. (2020) build on work by De Stefano (2016) to propose a classification of gig work into three distinct variants: app-work; crowdwork; and capital platform work.

App-work

App-work is perhaps the most commonly recognised and widely debated form of labour in the gig economy. App-work refers to service-providing intermediary digital platform organisations that utilise workers to perform tasks locally (e.g. transportation, food delivery, home repair) for customers who pay for these services, with the organisation retaining a percentage of the exchange (De Stefano, 2016; Duggan et al., 2020). This variant gets it title from the use of smartphone apps (short for "application") – software programs designed to perform a specific function directly for the user – in facilitating both supply from "app-workers" and demand from customers (Dickinson et al., 2014). This labour form sees traditional working activities in local markets conducted through apps, managed by intermediary digital platform organisations that intervene in setting minimum quality standards of service and in the selection and management of individuals who perform the work (Duggan et al., 2020).

App-work operates in markets where activities are engaged via platform organisations, but generally performed offline, meaning this variant of gig work is more visible in local environs. Many of the world's "leading" platform organisations in the gig economy operate in the app-work domain, including Uber, Deliveroo, Postmates, and TaskRabbit. By completing tasks locally rather than remotely, app-workers must not only assume responsibility for operating costs and risks but must also conform to the temporal rhythms of customer demand in a specific region, city, or town at any given time (Vallas & Schor, 2020). Likewise, because app-workers are offered tasks to be completed locally at a specific location and time, they typically operate under the surveillance of an algorithm, which assigns work and ensures that workers meet the minimum performance standards set by the platform organisation (Meijerink & Keegan, 2019). The processes involved in monitoring and managing app-workers using algorithmic technologies – known collectively as algorithmic management – allow platform organisations to quickly identify and offer labour to individual workers, and to monitor the completion of each stage of the labour process (Anderson, 2016; Bader & Kaiser, 2019).

The unique, complex nature of the working relationship found in app-work is a particularly interesting area of study. The speed at which the working relationship is created, and the speed at which the same relationship can be terminated, is fascinating for its hyper-temporality, unlike most other forms of working arrangements. That is, many app-workers can be hired almost instantly once they have agreed to the terms and conditions set out by the platform organisation, and once they have uploaded the relevant documentation via the app (e.g. driving licence, proof of identity, and so on). For some app-workers, they must electronically accept the platform organisation's terms and conditions each time they log in to the app to pursue work opportunities or gigs. These terms and conditions, sometimes referred to as a "supplier agreement," outline working arrangements, remuneration details, and other information that may be found within a legal contract of employment in more conventional arrangements (Tran & Sokas, 2017). If app-workers fail to meet any of the minimum quality standards set out by the platform organisation – most of which are tracked and quantified by the algorithmic management function – they may be deactivated from the platform organisation, essentially terminating the working relationship with immediate effect and with seemingly little recourse (Kellogg et al., 2020).

The unique nature of this arrangement means that app-work relationships are not rooted in traditional employee–employer dyads, but instead feature multiple parties contributing to a dynamic exchange agreement between three, or sometimes four, individual parties (Duggan et al., 2020). The following example illustrates such an exchange agreement between four parties:

> Deliveroo describes itself as offering a service that links workers with partner restaurants to provide a food-delivery service to customers. A *customer* uses the Deliveroo app to order food from a participating restaurant or *supplier*. The *app* notifies the restaurant, which prepares the order. At the same time, the app notifies a registered courier or *worker* that a delivery from the restaurant to the customer is required. Thus, the four italicised parties indicate that this is a multi-party working relationship.
>
> (Duggan et al., 2020: 118)

Indeed, all app-work involves a minimum of three parties, with platform organisations facilitating and mediating transactions between workers, customers, and occasionally suppliers (e.g. partner restaurants, as per the example from Deliveroo above). These multiple parties are illustrated in Figure 2.2. It is the app, representative of the platform organisation, that connects and directs each party in the work arrangement, thereby functioning as a centralised mechanism governing the dynamics of this working relationship (Duggan et al., 2020).

Crowdwork

The second gig work variant that we identify is crowdwork. Although similar to app-work in that crowdworkers connect with customers to sell their services via digital platform organisations, the differentiating feature of crowdwork is that individuals complete these tasks remotely and entirely online (De Stefano, 2016). As such, this gig work form may be seen as offering the potential for a global talent marketplace. Workers engaged in crowdwork undertake human intelligence tasks that computers cannot

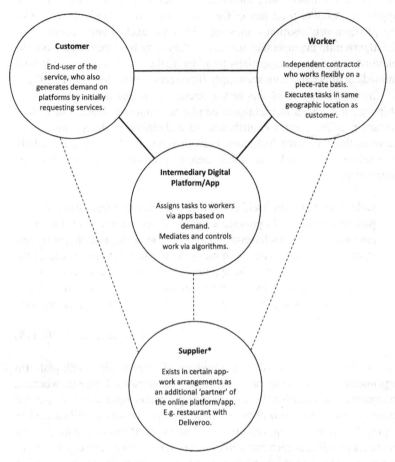

A broken line connects the supplier to other parties to indicate that the supplier only exists in certain app-working arrangements.

Figure 2.2 Parties involved in app-working arrangements, cited from Duggan et al. (2020)

perform, although these jobs generally require less training and experience than the work of cloud-based consultants or freelancers (Vallas & Schor, 2020). As a result, the nature of tasks completed by crowdworkers is quite varied and may include, for example, software coding, survey completion, audio transcription, or translation. Crowdwork can therefore be considered on a continuum from unskilled to highly skilled work. Examples of crowdwork organisations include Amazon Mechanical Turk, Fiverr, and Figure Eight.

In a typical crowdworking scenario, an external organisation or individual posts a task or project to be completed via a platform organisation. Any potential number of workers – referred to as the "crowd" – can attempt to undertake the task from any geographic location, with the most suitable individuals being selected (Berg, 2016). On some crowdworking platforms, individuals may work simultaneously on the same task, with the customer selecting and paying for only the best product (Duggan et al., 2020). Because crowdwork encompasses a large, highly varied group of workers competing for the same work opportunities, tasks are priced under extremely competitive conditions, and the ability to earn a living wage through crowdwork is typically limited (Panteli et al., 2020; Wood et al., 2019). Different crowdwork platforms set minimum compensation for certain tasks, whilst others let the compensation be set by their requester. In other cases, no clear relationship exists between the customer and the worker: they complete the task autonomously and are paid by the platform, which then provides the result to the customer. Despite the moderate to low earning potential, crowdwork has proved popular for both workers and customers. For example, figures show that 10,000 new tasks are published and 7,500 are completed per hour on Amazon Mechanical Turk (Berg, 2016).

From the perspective of user organisations or clients, crowdwork boasts the potential to cheaply disperse work that was once performed in-house, particularly for quick tasks that do not require significant instruction or supervision (De Stefano, 2016). In fact, crowdwork has become part of the organisational model for some firms, with a renowned example being a publishing company who has become one of Amazon Mechanical Turk's largest users by sourcing its entire labour force via the platform (Berg, 2016).

Crowdwork can also be advantageous for workers, primarily by allowing individuals to conveniently access work from anywhere in the world, provided there is an Internet connection, with the opportunity to utilise existing skills to earn additional income (Liu & Sundar, 2018). Yet, crowdwork is also characterised by the insecurity that accompanies all gig work, perhaps even more so than app-work, as it is often viewed as the completion of "micro-tasks" rather than "real" work, and thus, not meriting any traditional labour protections. Similarly, research has also reported that crowdworkers are left frustrated with the low level of pay, the lack of a reliable and steady source of work, the unresponsiveness of platform organisations to their concerns, and the poor, sometimes abusive, relationship with clients (Berg, 2016). This micro-task form may be viewed as the most commodified form of gig work labour.

While crowdwork is generally conceptualised as one form of work, it can be subdivided into different types (Howcroft & Bergvall-Kåreborn, 2019; Schmidt, 2017). Howcroft and Bergvall-Kåreborn (2019) provide a means to capture this heterogeneity by providing a typology of four types of crowdwork:

1. Online task crowdwork is a requester-initiated type of paid work for the completion of online tasks which can range from the micro-level to more complex projects. MTurk, UpWork, Fiverr would all fall under this categorisation.
2. "Playbour" crowdwork is also requester-initiated but represents a more speculative or non-paid form, meaning that it does not offer much by way of ongoing financial viability. It is becoming more common in software development where online crowdworkers look to provide creative solutions to problems that are set by requesters who pay a fee to the platform. Cash prizes may be provided to those best evaluated.
3. Asset-based services are viewed as worker-initiated that offer paid work for locally based transactions. The authors see this type of crowdwork as including platform organisations such as Airbnb, Uber, and TaskRabbit. Given the delineated features and characteristics of app-work and capital platform, set out within this chapter, we are not in agreement with this, Howcroft and Bergvall-Kåreborn's (2019), categorisation.
4. Profession-based freelancers is a type of worker-initiated, unpaid, or speculative work. This is highly specialist and skilled crowdwork which may, for example, include developing Android or Apple apps. Payment is only like to result where the developed product or service is sold to consumers.

While we disagree with Howcroft and Bergvall-Kåreborn's (2019) conceptualisation of capital platform work and app-work as asset-based services, we are supportive of the ideal in distinguishing crowdwork into distinct variants to emphasise that crowdwork is not a homogenous concept in itself. Rather, we see three key types of crowdwork which are separate to our additional gig-working classification:

- *Cloud-based* crowdwork is where tasks can be completed remotely via the Internet. If the task is not given to a specific individual but to an undefined group of people online, it is crowdwork.
- If the task is further subdivided into smaller units for piecemeal work, with each individual remunerated with an equally small amount of money, it is *micro-tasking* crowdwork.

- If tasks cannot be subdivided but work is carried out simultaneously, by a large group of individuals, while in the end only one result is used and paid for, it is *contest-based* crowdwork.

As all these types of crowdwork allow for the completion of tasks remotely, thereby lacking a discernible employer, it seems less likely that these workers will develop a transparent working relationship with the platform organisation (Duggan et al., 2020).

Capital platform work

Our final gig work variant – capital platform work – exists where individuals use digital platform organisations to sell goods peer-to-peer or to lease assets. Examples of capital platform organisations include Airbnb, where individuals may lease out accommodation, and Etsy, where individuals may buy and sell handmade, craft, or vintage items (the term is an acronym for "easy to sell yourself"). The focus on connecting customers with a form of capital owned by the individual, rather than the completion of labour, is a distinguishing feature of capital platform work in comparison with previously discussed gig work forms (Duggan et al., 2020).

The term "sharing economy," often used interchangeably with the gig economy, is most closely associated with capital platform work. This is because capital platform work relies on the "sharing" of underutilised assets, such as accommodation, for financial gain, rather than the completion of work (Schmidt, 2017). Consequently, the arrangement between capital platform workers and the platform organisation is more akin to an e-commerce or business-to-business relationship. This is sometimes referred to as a form of micro-entrepreneurship, in that these "workers" share greater similarities with small businesses than employees (Vandaele, 2018; Zervas et al., 2017). Notably, the role of algorithmic management in capital platform work appears to be much less pervasive, although the topic has received some limited scholarly attention (Cheng & Foley, 2019). The negative aspects of reliance on algorithmic mechanisms seem to be more pronounced in app-work and crowdwork, where there is a clear labour process to be completed, while the positive aspects seem to be more noticeable on capital platforms (Gerwe & Silva, 2020).

As with app-work and crowdwork, capital platform work is extremely popular with "workers" and customers. For example, Airbnb is now bigger than the world's top five hotel brands combined and has over four million listings in 100,000 cities across the globe (Airbnb, 2021). Yet, the platform organisation itself neither owns nor directly offers any physical accommodation – they simply offer technology that facilitates access to individuals who do, then charge a fee for the provision of the service (Gerwe & Silva, 2020). Likewise, while Airbnb does not directly employ any of its accommodation hosts, the organisation has invested significantly in creating a community and a sense of partnership with hosts via the sharing of best practices at so-called "host conventions" (Sundararajan, 2014).

Challenging gig workers' classification: Assembly Bill 5 and Proposition 22

Although this chapter has predominantly focused on identifying and clarifying the most significant classification issues in gig work, it should be noted that there also exists a burgeoning academic, practitioner, and press narrative surrounding the various legal challenges on these same issues (Stewart & Stanford, 2017; Wright et al., 2017). While we are unable to detail the multitude of cases being taken by gig workers across different jurisdictions and involving several platform organisations, we wish to briefly outline a recent, well-publicised example.

In September 2019, California adopted new legislation – Assembly Bill 5 (AB5) – aimed at preventing the misclassification of workers. Under this legislation, workers could only be classified as independent contractors when they pass the "ABC" test, which determines whether they are truly independent and free from all control and direction of the hiring company (McNicholas & Poydock, 2019). Workers who did not meet all conditions of this test would instead be classified as employees for the purposes of most major labour protections and benefits. AB5 was particularly influential for app-workers, who, under this legislation, essentially stood to gain either greater control over their roles via the eradication of the algorithmic management function, or greater security and benefits by becoming employees of the platform organisation. The former was mostly realised when AB5 came into effect: for example, rideshare platform organisations allowed workers to view end-destinations prior to accepting tasks; penalties for rejecting tasks were removed; and workers gained more control over setting payment rates (Campbell, 2020).

However, the pushback on AB5 from platform organisations was significant and noteworthy. Before long, the controversies surrounding AB5 became so intense that California's gig economy – primarily led by the major rideshare organisations – funded a ballot initiative, Proposition 22, which sought to fully exempt gig workers from AB5. In backing this initiative, platform organisations collectively spent over $200 million on the "Yes on 22" campaign, which targeted both workers and customers every time they used the services of the associated platform organisations (Hussain et al., 2020). The argument of platform organisations was relatively simple: AB5 will end the gig economy by increasing costs, both for organisations and for end-user customers, and will eradicate workers' flexibility. Yet, the wider argument was less simple and the initiative quickly became hugely controversial, being viewed as a high-stakes battle between corporate power and workers' rights.

Ultimately, in November 2020, Proposition 22 was successfully passed in California. For the most part, reaction to the outcome of AB5 and Proposition 22 has been mixed. A spokesperson for the "Yes on 22" campaign noted that the gig economy's win "represents the future of work in an increasingly technologically-driven economy" (Conger, 2020). Likewise, Uber's chief executive said that the passing of Proposition 22 means "the future of independent work is more secure" (Hawkins, 2020), before outlining plans to advocate for similar legislation across the United States. Yet, for those of the view that the app-workers' independent contractor status was inappropriate, the passing of Proposition 22 signalled a major defeat. Perceptions and perspectives aside, the AB5-Proposition 22 debacle clearly highlighted the strength and influence of the gig economy and the colossal scale of the challenges faced by governments and legislators in attempting to regulate work in this domain.

Conclusion

This chapter has summarised the key worker-classification issues that exist in the gig economy. In doing so, we have sought to depart from monolithic perspectives by focusing on two key areas: distinguishing gig work as a new type of contingent labour; and delineating gig work itself into three key variants. Contingent work represents a range of alternatives to traditional employment, many of which bear similarities to gig work. However, these work arrangements are also unique in their own right, consisting of important nuances and features (Cappelli & Keller, 2013). Likewise, gig work, with its reliance on advanced algorithmic technologies and digital platforms, represents a novel work form. Consequently, it is erroneous to simply subsume gig work into an extension of existing types of contingent work. Instead, gig work exists within the domain of contingent work, but stands alone as a distinctive form of labour.

Just as gig work should not be subsumed into existing types of contingent work, it is equally important to recognise that gig work itself is not homogenous. Gig economy scholarship has often failed to distinguish

Table 2.1 Summary of key papers that delineate the heterogeneity of gig work

Source	Key contribution
De Stefano (2016)	Paper considers the labour dimensions of the gig economy suggesting that it represents a broadening of non-standard employment forms and increases the informalisation and casualisation of work. Paper also sets out two distinct gig work variants: "crowdwork" and "work-on-demand via apps."
Duggan et al. (2020)	Proposes a classification of gig work into three variants all of which are based around technological aspects: "crowdwork," "app-work," and "capital platform work." Paper then focuses on app-work and critically discusses the role of algorithmic management before providing a future research agenda.
Howcroft & Bergvall-Kåreborn (2019)	Paper proposes a typology of crowdwork, namely, "online task crowdwork," "playbour crowdwork," "asset-based services," and "profession-based freelance crowdwork."

between variants of gig work (see Table 2.1 for key papers that delineate different types), instead using the term as an all-encompassing moniker to capture all types of precarious work where digital platform organisations are involved. We argue that this conceptualisation is oversimplified, and fails to consider the distinctive features and issues found across the very broad range of platform organisations in the gig economy. Thus, we outline recent research which proposes the classification of gig work into three key variants: app-work (De Stefano, 2016; Duggan et al., 2020); crowdwork (De Stefano, 2016; Duggan et al., 2020; Howcroft & Bergvall-Kåreborn, 2019) which can be further broken down into multiple types; and capital platform work (Duggan et al., 2020). Understanding that gig work exists in these various forms is a crucial step in effectively identifying and addressing the most pertinent issues that exist in the gig economy, and in appropriately understanding the varied experiences of different types of gig workers. Each work variant represents a different set of challenges and opportunities, which can only be fully appreciated when first viewed in isolation.

References

Airbnb (2021). *About us*. https://news.airbnb.com/about-us/.
Anderson, D.N. (2016). Wheels in the head: Ridesharing as monitored performance. *Surveillance & Society*, 14 (2): 240–258.

Ashford, S.J., George, E., & Blatt, R. (2007). Old assumptions, new work: The opportunities and challenges of research on nonstandard employment. *Academy of Management Annals*, 1 (1): 65–117.

Bader, V., & Kaiser, S. (2019). Algorithmic decision-making? The user interface and its role for human involvement in decisions supported by artificial intelligence. *Organization*, 26 (5): 655–672.

Barley, S.R., Bechky, B.A., & Milliken, F.J. (2017). The changing nature of work: Careers, identities, and work lives in the 21st century. *Academy of Management Discoveries*, 3 (2): 111–115.

Berg, J. (2016). Income security in the on-demand economy: Findings and policy lessons from a survey of crowdworkers. *ILO: Conditions of Work and Employment Series No. 74*, 1–33.

Bernhardt, A., & Thomason, S. (2017). *What Do We Know About Gig Work in California? An Analysis of Independent Contracting*. UC Berkeley Labour Centre. California, USA.

Bidwell, M. Briscoe, F., Fernandez-Mateo, I., & Sterling, A. (2013). The employment relationship and inequality: How and why changes in employment practices are reshaping rewards in organizations. *Academy of Management Annals*, 7 (1): 61–121.

Birgillito, G., & Birgillito, M. (2018). Algorithms and ratings: Tools to manage labour relations – proposals to renegotiate labour conditions for platform drivers. *Labour & Law Issues*, 4 (2): 26–50.

Bonet, R., Cappelli, P., & Hamori, M. (2013). Labour market intermediaries and the new paradigm for human resources. *Academy of Management Annals*, 7 (1): 341–392.

Boudreau, J., Jesuthasan, R., & Creelman, D. (2015). *Lead the Work: Navigating a World Beyond Employment*. Wiley, San Francisco.

Bryson, J.R. (2018). Divisions of labour, technology and the transformation of work: Workers to robot or self-employment and the gig economy. In A. Paasi, J. Harrison, & M. Jones (Eds.), *Handbook on the Geographies of Regions and Territories*. Edward Elgar, London. 141–152.

Campbell, H. (2020). Everything you should know about AB5 and its impact on Uber. *The Rideshare Guy*, 7 October.

Cappelli, P., & Keller, J.R. (2013). Classifying work in the new economy. *Academy of Management Review*, 38 (4): 575–596.

Cappelli, P., Bassi, L., Katz, H., Knoke, D., Osterman, P., & Useem, M. (1997). *Change at Work*. Oxford University Press, New York.

Carr, C.T., Hall, R.D., Mason, A.J., & Varney, E.J. (2017). Cueing employability in the gig economy: Effects of task-relevant and task-irrelevant information on Fiverr. *Management Communication Quarterly*, 31 (3): 409–428.

Cheng, M., & Foley, C. (2019). Algorithmic management: The case of Airbnb. *International Journal of Hospitality Management*, 83: 33–36.

Cochrane, R., & McKeown, T. (2015). Vulnerability and agency work: From the workers' perspectives. *International Journal of Manpower*, 36 (6): 947–965.

Collier, R.B., Dubal, V.B., & Carter, C. (2017). Labour platforms and gig work: The failure to regulate. *Institute for Research on Labour and Employment: Working Paper 106-17*.

Conger, K. (2020). Uber and Lyft drivers in California will remain contractors. *The New York Times*, 4 November.

Connelly, C.E., & Gallagher, D.G. (2004). Emerging trends in contingent work research. *Journal of Management*, 30 (6): 959–983.

De Stefano, V. (2016). The rise of the "just-in-time" workforce: On-demand work, crowdwork and labour protection in the gig economy. *International Labour Office: Conditions of Work and Employment Series*, 71.

Dickinson, J.E., Ghali, K., Cherrett, T., Speed, C., Davies, N., & Norgate, S. (2014). Tourism and the smartphone app: Capabilities, emerging practice and scope in the travel domain. *Current Issues in Tourism*, 17 (1): 84–101.

Donnelly, R. (2008). Careers and temporal flexibility in the new economy: An Anglo-Dutch comparison of the organisation of consultancy work. *Human Resource Management Journal*, 18 (3): 197–215.

Duggan, J., Sherman, U., Carbery, R., & McDonnell, A. (2020). Algorithmic management and app-work in the gig economy: A research agenda for employment relations and HRM. *Human Resource Management Journal*, 30 (1): 114–132.

Dundon, T. & Rafferty, A. (2018). The (potential) demise of HRM? *Human Resource Management Journal*, 28: 377–391.

Etzioni, A. (2018). Benefits for gig workers. *Challenge*, 61 (3): 255–268.

Felstead, A., & Jewson, N. (1999). Flexible labour and non-standard employment: An agenda of issues. In A. Felstead & N. Jewson (Eds.), *Global Trends in Flexible Labour*. Macmillan, London, 1–20.

Finegold, D., Levenson, A., & van Buren, M. (2005). Access to training and its impact on temporary workers. *Human Resource Management Journal*, 15 (2): 66–85.

Fisher, S.L., & Connelly, C.E. (2017). Lower cost or just lower value? Modelling the organisational costs and benefits of contingent work. *Academy of Management Discoveries*, 3 (2): 165–186.

Friedman, G. (2014). Workers without employers: Shadow corporations and the rise of the gig economy. *Review of Keynesian Economics*, 2 (2): 171–188.

Fynes, B., Morrissey, T., Roche, W.K., Whelan, B.J., & Williams, J. (1996). *Flexible Working Lives: The Changing Nature of Working Time Arrangements in Ireland*. Oak Tree Press, Dublin.

Gandini, A. (2019). Labour process theory and the gig economy. *Human Relations*, 72 (6): 1039–1056.

Geller, J., & Mazor, A.H. (2011). *Global Business Driven HR Transformation: The Journey Continues*. Deloitte.

Gerwe, O., & Silva, R. (2020). Clarifying the sharing economy: Conceptualization, typology, antecedents, and effects. *Academy of Management Perspectives*, 34 (1): 65–96.

Ghosh, D., Willinger, G.L., & Ghosh, S. (2009). A firm's external environment and the hiring of a non-standard workforce: Implications for organisations. *Human Resource Management Journal*, 19 (4): 433–453.

Gramano, E. (2019). Digitalisation and work: Challenges from the platform economy. *Contemporary Social Science*, 15 (4): 476–488.

Guest, D.E. (2004). The psychology of the employment relationship: An analysis based on the psychological contract. *Applied Psychology*, 53 (4): 541–555.

Harris, S.D., & Krueger, A.B. (2015). *A Proposal for Modernising Labour Laws for Twenty-First-Century Work: The "Independent Worker."* The Hamilton Project. Washington DC, USA.

Harvey, G., Rhodes, C., Vachhani, S.J., & Williams, K. (2017). Neo-villeiny and the service sector: The case of hyper flexible and precarious work in fitness centres. *Work, Employment and Society*, 31 (1): 19–35.

Hawkins, A.J. (2020). Uber takes a victory lap on Prop 22 and talks about taking it national. *The Verge*, 5 November.

Helfen, M. (2015). Institutionalising precariousness? The politics of boundary work in legalising agency work in Germany, 1949–2004. *Organization Studies*, 36 (10): 1387–1422.

Howcroft, D., & Bergvall-Kåreborn, B. (2019). A typology of crowdwork platforms. *Work, Employment and Society*, 33 (1): 21–38.

Hurley, J. (2018). Boss determined to deliver the right ingredients for success. *The Times*, 26 February.

Hussain, S., Bhuiyan, J., & Menezes, R. (2020). How Uber and Lyft persuaded California to vote their way. *Los Angeles Times*, 13 November.

Inkson, K., Gunz, H., Ganesh, S., & Roper, J. (2012). Boundaryless careers: Bringing back boundaries. *Organization Studies*, 33 (3): 323–340.

International Labour Office (2016). *Non-Standard Employment Around the World: Understanding Challenges, Shaping Prospects*. ILO, Geneva.

Kalleberg, A.L. (2000). Nonstandard employment relations: Part-time, temporary and contract work, *Annual Review of Sociology*, 26: 341–365.

Kalleberg, A.L. (2012). Job quality and precarious work: Clarifications, controversies, and challenges. *Work and Occupations*, 39 (4): 427–448.

Kellogg, K.C., Valentine, M.A., & Christin, A. (2020). Algorithms at work: The new contested terrain of control. *Academy of Management Annals*, 14 (1): 366–410.

Kroon, B., & Paauwe, J. (2013). Structuration of precarious employment in economically constrained firms: The case of Dutch agriculture. *Human Resource Management Journal*, 24 (1): 19–37.

Kuhn, K.M. (2016). The rise of the "Gig Economy" and implications for understanding work and workers. *Industrial and Organisational Psychology*, 9 (1): 157–162.

Kuhn, K.M., & Maleki, A. (2017). Micro-entrepreneurs, dependent contractors, and instaserfs: Understanding online labour platform workforces. *Academy of Management Perspectives*, 31 (3): 183–200.

Lambert, S.J. (2008). Passing the buck: Labour flexibility practices that transfer risk onto hourly workers. *Human Relations*, 61 (9): 1203–1227.

Lemmon, G., Wilson, M.S., Posig, M., & Glibkowski, B.C. (2016). Psychological contract development, distributive justice, and performance of independent contractors: The role of negotiation behaviours and the fulfilment of resources. *Journal of Leadership and Organisational Studies*, 23 (4): 424–439.

Liu, B., & Sundar, S. (2018). Microworkers as research participants: Does underpaying Turkers lead to cognitive dissonance? *Computers in Human Behavior*, 88: 61–69.

Madrigal, A.C. (2019). The Uber IPO is a landmark. *The Atlantic*.

McGaughey, E. (2018). Taylorooism: When network technology meets corporate power. *Industrial Relations Journal*, 49 (5–6): 459–472.

McLean Parks, J., Kiddler, D.L., & Gallagher, D.G. (1998). Fitting square pegs into round holes: Mapping the domain of contingent work arrangements onto the psychological contract. *Journal of Organisational Behavior*, 19: 697–730.

McNeill, J. (2019). Introducing lyft driver services. *Medium*, 26 March.

McNicholas, C., & Poydock, M. (2019). How California's AB5 protects workers from misclassification. *Economic Policy Institute*, 14 November.

Meijerink, J., & Keegan, A. (2019). Conceptualizing human resource management in the gig economy: Toward a platform ecosystem perspective. *Journal of Managerial Psychology*, 34 (4): 214–232.

O'Sullivan, M., Turner, T., McMahon, J., Ryan, L., Lavelle, J., Murphy, C., O'Brien, M., & Gunnigle, P. (2015). *A Study on the Prevalence of Zero Hours Contracts Among Irish Employers and Their Impact on Employees*. Kemmy Business School, University of Limerick, Limerick, Ireland.

Panteli, N., Rapti, A., & Scholarios, D. (2020). "If he just knew who we were": Microworkers' emerging bonds of attachment in a fragmented employment relationship. *Work, Employment and Society*, 34 (3): 476–494.

Rosenberg, S., & Lapidus, J. (1999). Contingent and non-standard work in the United States: Towards a more poorly compensated, insecure workforce. In A. Felstead & N. Jewson (Eds.), *Global Trends in Flexible Labour*. Macmillan, London, 62–83.

Rozzi, F. (2018). The impact of the gig economy on US labour markets: Understanding the role of non-employer firms using econometric models and the example of Uber. *Junior Management Science*, 3 (2): 33–56.

Schein, E.H. (1980). *Organisational Psychology*. Prentice Hall, Englewood Cliffs, NJ.

Schmidt, F.A. (2017). *Digital Labour Markets in the Platform Economy: Mapping the Political Challenges of Crowd Work and Gig Work*. Friedrich-Ebert-Stiftung. Berlin, Germany.

Smith, R., & Leberstein, S. 2015. *Rights on Demand: Ensuring Workplace Standards and Worker Security in the On-Demand Economy*. National Employment Law Project, New York.

Spreitzer, G.M., Cameron, L., & Garrett, L. (2017). Alternative work arrangements: Two images of the new world of work. *Annual Review of Organizational Psychology and Organizational Behavior*, 4: 473–499.

Stewart, A., & Stanford, J. (2017). Regulating work in the gig economy: What are the options? *The Economic and Labour Relations Review*, 28 (3): 420–437.

Sundararajan, A. (2014). What Airbnb gets about culture that Uber doesn't. *Harvard Business Review*, 27 November.

Taylor, M., Marsh, G., Nicol, D., & Broadbent, P. (2017) *Good Work: The Taylor Review of Modern Working Practices*. London: Department of Business, Energy and Industrial.

Todolí-Signes, A. (2017). The gig economy: Employee, self-employed or the need for a special employment regulation? *Transfer: European Review of Labour and Research*, 23 (2): 193–205.

Tran, M., & Sokas, R.K. (2017). The gig economy and contingent work: An occupational health assessment. *Journal of Occupational and Environmental Medicine*, 59 (4): 63–66.

Uber (2019). *Company Information*.

Vallas, S., & Schor, J.B. (2020). What do platforms do? Understanding the gig economy. *Annual Review of Sociology*, 46.

Vandaele, K. (2018). *Will Trade Unions Survive in the Platform Economy? Emerging Patterns of Platform Workers' Collective Voice and Representation in Europe*. Working Paper, European Trade Union Institute.

Ward, K., Grimshaw, D., Rubery, J., & Beynon, H. (2001). Dilemmas in the management of temporary work agency staff. *Human Resource Management Journal*, 11 (4): 3–21.

Weil, D. (2017). How to make employment fair in an age of contracting and temp work. *Harvard Business Review*, 24 March.

Wolfe, J.H. (1941). Determination of employer-employee relationships in social legislation. *Columbia Law Review*, 41 (6): 1015–1037.

Wood, A.J. (2016). Flexible scheduling, degradation of job quality and barriers to collective voice. *Human Relations*, 69 (10): 1989–2010.

Wood, A.J., Graham, M., Lehdonvirta, V., & Hjorth, I. (2019). Good gig, bad gig: Autonomy and algorithmic control in the global gig economy. *Work, Employment and Society*, 33 (1): 56–75.

Wright, C.F., Wailes, N., Bamber, G.J., & Lansbury, R.D. (2017). Beyond national systems, towards a "gig economy"? A research agenda for international and comparative employment relations. *Employee Responsibilities and Rights Journal*, 29 (4): 247–257.

Zervas, G., Proserpio, D., & Byers, J.W. (2017). The rise of the sharing economy: Estimating the impact of Airbnb on the hotel industry. *Journal of Marketing Research*, 54 (5): 687–705.

3   Technology, algorithms, and digital platform organisations

Introduction

It is increasingly recognised across research and practice that technological innovations play a key role in the world of work. More pointedly, technological advancements are central to creating, structuring, and facilitating a new labour market in the form of the gig economy. The foremost defining characteristic of the gig economy is that it offers digital platforms or applications that connect individuals seeking services with those providing services. As a result, the platform organisation itself is recognised as a technology company rather than a service provider (Tran & Sokas, 2017). In many ways, the role of technology here appears simplistic, yet strikingly innovative. For platform organisations, technology is at the core of every part of their operations. For customers, the technologies offered by platform organisations grant unprecedently fast and convenient access to various market services (Frost, 2017).

Yet, for gig workers – the party who directly provide the services on offer – the role of technology is more complex. While undoubtedly creating exciting new opportunities to work independently and away from the confines of a traditional office environment, literature also tells us that gig workers are on the receiving end of the more intense and perhaps detrimental capabilities of such advanced technologies (Kuhn & Maleki, 2017; Wood et al., 2019). Thus, the autonomy promise offered by gig work which lures in many appears to be more bounded and constrained in practice.

The pervasiveness of technology in gig work is most effectively illustrated by the algorithmic technologies which are embedded in platform organisations. The processes enabled by these algorithmic technologies – known collectively as algorithmic management – allow platform organisations to manage and allocate work tasks, closely monitor gig workers' activities, and to generate individualised performance metrics. Importantly, the governing role of algorithmic management is more extreme within

DOI: 10.4324/9780429351488-3

certain variants of gig work, and even within some organisations, with the starkest examples perhaps being the immediate "deactivation" of certain types of gig workers whom the algorithm determines to have failed to meet oblique minimum performance standards (Duggan et al., 2020).

In this chapter, we examine the technological trends and developments underpinning the rise of the gig economy, with a particular focus on the digitalisation of work in this context. In doing so, we place a particular focus on the role of the algorithmic management function by considering the criticality of this relatively novel and alternative means of manipulating technology to monitor, manage, and control gig workers. We analyse the growing body of literature on algorithmic management to illustrate the breadth of the processes enabled by these technologies and, through the use of practical examples, we illustrate how these mechanisms are utilised across different variants of gig work. Finally, towards the close of the chapter, we present a summary of the various types of control strategies enabled by the algorithmic management function across the gig work variants identified in Chapter 2.

Key chapter takeaways

- Technological advancements and the increasing digitalisation of work have been crucial in enabling the formation and continued growth of the gig economy.
- Advanced algorithmic technologies have become increasingly pervasive in facilitating a novel type of workforce management – known as algorithmic management – within the gig economy.
- The various functions and processes of the algorithmic management function may be used to monitor, mediate, and control the activities of gig workers.
- For the most part, the algorithmic management function lacks transparency, and gig workers largely appear to lack in-depth understanding of how this tool is used in managing their labour efforts.

The increasing digitalisation of work

Throughout history, work has typically been geographically bounded. That is, employees and the work that they perform have been inextricably linked, with the completion of the labour process itself being the most place-bound of all factors of production (Graham et al., 2017). However, the widespread advancement of technology and subsequent use of the internet have changed this. Much of the world is now characterised by rapidly changing connectivity. In the last decade alone, the percentage of humanity connected to the internet has almost tripled, and there are now over three billion "connected" people globally (Graham et al., 2017). As a result, workers, clients, managers, and consumers of work have the ability to be remotely located at different corners of the world.

More specifically, in the context of labour, technological advancements have engendered a wide array of transformations, often affecting the ways in which work activities are carried out and spatially organised (Aroles et al., 2019). The workplace is no longer solely associated with the "four walls" of an office or factory floor. Throughout the last decade, organisations have increasingly deployed technologies designed to parse through large amounts of data, acquire skills and knowledge, and operate autonomously (Wang et al., 2020). These technologies have enabled workers to link directly with customers for the provision of services, with potentially large gains in the quality, speed, and efficiency of service (Harris & Krueger, 2015). For organisations, the same technological innovation has played an important role in creating novel, comprehensive surveillance and control systems to advance workforce management capabilities (Hall, 2010) and shifting more transactional risks to the individual. In fact, literature argues that understanding how strategies of managerial control have evolved with the advent of new technologies is key to understanding the future of workplace relations, although there is also a recognition that there remains a significant lack of detailed insight regarding the effects and implications of these technologies (Ivanova et al., 2018; Schafheitle et al., 2020).

Consequently, an important consideration when examining the increasing digitalisation of work is to take societal as well as economic perspectives into account. In other words, in recognising the superior features of these technologies for transactional efficiency and service, it is crucial that the success and expansion of business models incorporating these technologies is not to the detriment of the individuals involved nor wider society (Harris & Krueger, 2015). Our smartphones and devices have become, in a relatively short period of time, sources of whole worlds of communication, information, and potential employment opportunities (Frost, 2017). Yet, an often-cited consequence of the rise of this so-called "app age" is the formidable challenge created for legislative bodies as they struggle to keep pace with technological disruption, with the obvious fear being that every role will eventually be transformed, at least to some extent, into a freelance activity where technology acts simultaneously as a mediator and outsourcing tool (Maselli et al., 2016). Given that gig workers are not normally covered under existing legislative protections, nor in receipt of benefits such as sick pay, critical illness cover, and so on, there is a real need to develop a revised or new social contract that better accounts for this future of work.

It is difficult to decipher whether the creators and implementors of new technologies in the workplace intentionally or unintentionally alter the nature of work and forms of organising, or whether organisations and institutions naturally morph and transform as the world changes. According to Barley et al. (2017), both of these dynamics occur, and regardless of which dynamic takes precedence, the key issue lies in recognising the reality of these changes and subsequent social consequences. While reflecting on the implementation of existing technologies is an important starting point in doing this, we also exercise caution that the rapid pace at which these technologies have emerged has not halted, but instead continues to accelerate. For example, developments in automation and artificial intelligence are regular features in discussions on the future of work – both in the context of how such trends help businesses to do more with less and provide better results, as well as the obvious challenges posed for employees who need to change how they work in line with such innovations (Wilburn & Wilburn, 2018).

Likewise, the unprecedented disruption of working life as caused by the COVID-19 pandemic has seen organisations and industries across all regions become ever more reliant on online connectivity. Throughout 2020, the acceleration of change prompted by this disruption was so noteworthy that a study conducted by McKinsey (2020) indicates that response efforts to the pandemic in the business community sped up the adoption of digital technologies by several years, with results representing a quantum leap at both organisation and industry levels when compared to pre-COVID-19 studies. Noteworthy also was how the category of "essential worker" emerged during the COVID-19 pandemic and how many gig workers were included in this classification, yet the lack of social protections afforded to them was also evident.

In the context of gig work

Although our discussion of technological trends in the workplace could easily spawn a lengthier account, we return our focus once more to examining the nature of these trends and issues in the specific context of gig work. In the gig economy, much of the technological innovation is embodied in digital platform organisations themselves, with this unique component of the labour market being built upon virtual infrastructures. Through their very purpose, they change the way people work by creating novel digital task marketplaces that supply on-demand services (Rozzi, 2018).

As illustrated in greater depth in Chapter 2, the services offered are varied: they can be entirely online, incorporating a range of remote micro-tasks; or offline, consisting of a diverse spectrum of in-person services such as transportation or food delivery (Tran & Sokas, 2017). In all cases, the unique characteristic is that technology, in some capacity, enables the occurrence of all transactions in gig work. Within these digital marketplaces, platform organisations act as intermediaries between two or more parties that could not easily interact otherwise (McIntyre et al., 2020). Consequently, human interaction is greatly reduced, or even eliminated in some scenarios, with workers structurally operating at the other side of a screen based on the demand created by requestors or customers. Thus, literature has described gig work as contributing to the creation of a new group of "invisible workers" – where workers operate in a new, hyper-flexible fashion, and through new technologies, to the extent that the actual completion of labour may be susceptible to dehumanisation, at least from the perspective of customers (De Stefano, 2016).

Consequently, the pervasiveness of technology in gig work is a consistent debate across literature, with an increasing number of conceptual and empirical studies seeking to conceptualise and characterise the precise nature of the technologies used, and the subsequent implications for the working relationship (e.g. Duggan et al., 2020; Veen et al., 2020; Wood et al., 2019). At the heart of this debate is the potential for the algorithmic technologies used by organisations to intensely monitor, mediate, and control gig workers' activities – which, if accurate, moves towards invalidating the notion that gig workers are independent contractors who work autonomously, rather than employees who operate under the control of the form (Frost, 2017). In ensuring quality control and customer satisfaction, platform organisations are known to set minimum quality standards for gig workers, and to take corrective action if algorithmic tracking mechanisms or customer ratings determine that those standards have not been met (Jabagi et al., 2019).

This viewpoint starkly contrasts with the perspective of platform organisations, who position themselves as technology companies who simply provide a digital platform to connect supply and demand in particular markets. This attempted positioning has typically received harsh criticism by many scholars and commentators, with arguments that the utilisation of algorithmic technologies is simply a "fig leaf" to conceal old methods of worker exploitation, wherein working standards are fragmented and whole jobs are disintegrated into on-demand tasks without the safety nets that accompany traditional employment (Healy et al., 2017). Subsequently, the gig economy has been accused of establishing a new type of modern-day, scientific management: so-called "digital Taylorism," where technology is used to break jobs into smaller tasks and to measure everything that workers do, sometimes giving bonuses to high-performers and deactivating those on the opposite end of the scale (Duggan et al., 2020; McGaughey, 2018).

Algorithms and gig work

The increasing presence of algorithmic technologies in gig work, and indeed, the ever-developing capabilities of these technologies in managing large workforces, forms an ongoing and important area of interest and discussion across researchers and policymakers. By helping to create a cyber-coordinated labour market, the advanced algorithms used by platform organisations provide the tools to intensify, accelerate, and expand the market for contract labour (Collier et al., 2017).

Algorithms are defined as computational formulae that have the ability to autonomously make decisions based on statistical models or decisions rules without explicit human intervention (Eurofound, 2018). Without delving too far into literature on IT systems and processes, it is important to understand that algorithms operate based on a sequence of instructions telling a computer what to do, within a set of precisely defined steps and rules, in order to efficiently accomplish a task (Lee et al., 2015). However, instead of remaining static by repeatedly processing a stable set of consistent instructions, algorithms can instead "learn" to rewrite themselves as they work. With this innovative self-learning functionality, algorithms can process tremendous amounts of information and transactions (i.e. data) instantaneously, taking a vast number of variables into account and determining an appropriate response based on learned rules (Hyers & Kovacova, 2018). In this way, algorithms have quickly been recognised as enabling organisations to convert computing power into a novel, dynamic digitalised economic tool (Kenney & Zsyman, 2016). Thus, the innovation enabled by algorithms forms the very foundation of the gig economy.

With their advanced capabilities, algorithms are presented as objectively and mathematically correct by autonomously managing business processes and learning to solve problems in increasingly complex domains – and, as a result, people are encouraged to trust and abide by them (Lee et al., 2015; Mann & O'Neill, 2016). Within organisations, this has seen algorithms increasingly make decisions that have tended to previously be the remit of managers and HR professionals. For example, the algorithms found on hiring platforms, such as LinkedIn, can sort through thousands of profiles to help identify the most promising job candidates to company recruiters (Carey & Smith, 2016). Likewise, in the gig economy, platform organisations are built upon algorithms that enable the matching of customers with workers, while also functioning to evaluate the performance of gig workers in many cases (Duggan et al., 2020; Rosenblat, 2018). As a result, platform organisations can more easily exonerate themselves from any responsibility or culpability with respect to managing their workforce, by appealing to algorithms to essentially dissolve their authority into the objective, disinterested medium of a software programme (van Doorn, 2017).

However, the transparency of the algorithms upon which these digitalised management processes are based has repeatedly been called into question, raising significant ethical considerations around these practices (Vandaele, 2018). At a foundational level, it has been argued that algorithms – as purely technological agents – lack the emotional intelligence and moral authenticity of human managers (Jago, 2019). Likewise, from a labour perspective, the wholly digital organisation of much gig work has also faced criticism. In their current form, many platform organisations are depicted as algorithmic, non-negotiable employers who indirectly hold all control over the labour process by governing the "rules of the game" to suit their own strategic objectives (Kim et al., 2018; Vandaele, 2018). As Lehdonvirta (2018) notes, for gig workers the fickle algorithm is the new source of workplace tyranny.

Algorithmic management

The algorithmic processes and mechanisms used to monitor, coordinate, and control the activities of gig workers are referred to, collectively, as algorithmic management. Defined as a system of control where self-learning algorithms are given the responsibility for making and executing decisions affecting labour (Duggan et al., 2020), algorithmic management effectively limits human involvement and oversight of the labour process. Sizable quantities of data are continuously generated and accumulated, based on transactions and workers' activities (Eurofound, 2018), with this data then being used to train algorithms to replace some of the tasks and processes that workers typically engage with. Consequently, workers and consumers contribute, unremunerated, to the stock of intangible capital of the platform. This has seen stratospheric valuations placed on platform organisations, particularly in the app-work domain, with Lyft, for example, being valued at $24 billion at IPO in 2019 despite losing over $900 million in 2018 (Ovide, 2019).

For platform organisations, algorithmic management keeps marginal and labour costs relatively low (Schmidt, 2017), with significant savings arising from the use of algorithms as virtual automated managers, thus negating the need for human supervisors and managers (Lee et al., 2015). The functions of algorithmic management include, but are not limited to, setting expectations and minimum quality standards, tracking workers' activities, and disciplining workers who fail to meet performance expectations (Vandaele, 2018). Because these functions are automated, algorithmic management makes many decisions without human oversight or standard recourse opportunities, meaning the implementing of actions may often be to the detriment of gig workers' social protection. Consequently, through its very purpose of automating management practice, algorithmic management serves to eliminate the more interpersonal and empathetic aspects of people management within organisations. Without a human manager or organisation partner advocating the needs of workers and maintaining a balanced working relationship (Gilbert et al., 2011), individuals working on platform organisations seem less likely to build the trust, confidence, and overall improved sense of well-being that we associate with strong, commitment-oriented working relationships.

Yet, while algorithmic management appears to eradicate many of the features and norms that characterise traditional working relationships, the same technologies have also been described as being agentic, given their temporally embedded capacity to intentionally constrain, complement, and/ or substitute for humans in the practice of routines (Murray et al., 2020). Across different types of platform organisations, algorithmic technologies may be used to determine the eligibility of workers, to facilitate or restrict access to tasks, and to assess workers' performance via the accumulation of various metrics and feedback (Kuhn & Maleki, 2017).

In many varied ways, these technologies can fundamentally alter our understanding of workplace management by how they control the supply of labour, determine protocols, determine rules and guidelines for workers, make decisions, and encourage specific actions (Murray et al., 2020). The influence can also vary to more direct forms such as where platform organisations target workers with incentives or rewards or choose to remove or deactivate them from work opportunities without remedy.

In recent years, these issues have received increasing attention across literature, particularly in efforts to examine the implications of these practices for individual gig workers and for the study and practice of people management (Duggan et al., 2020; Meijerink et al., 2021). Although this is very much a developing area, existing discourse has broadly identified negative, or at the very least, concerning, implications (Panteli et al., 2020; Shanahan & Smith, 2021; Williams et al., 2021). In fact, even when knowledge and literature on algorithmic management was in its absolute infancy, the concept drew considerable criticism by being described as the "boss from hell" (Slee, 2017): erratic and bad-tempered with the potential to fire workers on a whim without recourse to appeal.

Algorithmic management: a new, comprehensive type of control?

Algorithmic management processes enable a level of surveillance that is not present in most workplaces, likely creating significant information and power asymmetries between gig workers and platform organisations

(Jarrahi et al., 2020). Accordingly, these mechanisms combine to form a strategic system of control, at once limiting the information that gig workers can access, placing incentives on compliance, and pressuring individuals to treat offers or prompts as commands (Griesbach et al., 2019). From this perspective, technology does not just enable platform organisations to simply create digital marketplaces – crucially, it also allows firms to closely regulate the markets that they create. Thus, the freedom and choice that is commonly promised and promoted as a key benefit of gig work is, in reality, often heavily constrained. As a result, the advanced control systems created by algorithmic management are all-encompassing – often described as "algocratic" (Aneesh, 2009) – where almost all forms of control or task allocation are ascribed to algorithmic activity (Rosenblat & Stark, 2016; Veen et al., 2020).

These systems, according to Wood et al. (2019), signify an absence of trust in the working relationship by ensuring that labour is appropriately carried out on the basis of the threat of discipline rather than on interpersonal relations of trust and collaboration. Studies have suggested that platform organisations' algorithmic control strategies, while ostensibly appearing subtle, are diverse and comprehensive, particularly where gamification and ranking systems are utilised (Gandini, 2018; Cheng & Foley, 2019). While these technologies may provide increased flexibility in where and when to work, the same technologies restrict autonomy by facilitating increased monitoring of workers and reducing control over their work (Norlander et al., 2021). This outcome potentially renders gig workers as unable to reap the benefits expected from working virtually and remotely, while also finding themselves trapped in a state of constant precariousness, comparable to a permanent probationary period (Kalleberg & Vallas, 2018).

Thus, while we may identify the increasing prevalence and disruption represented by algorithmic management, the specific nature and intricacies of the mechanisms implemented in gig work remain somewhat elusive (Wu et al., 2019). This is likely due to the incredibly broad scope of the processes and functions enabled by algorithmic management, and, importantly, the variability in the implementation of these mechanisms across variants of gig work, and even across different platform organisations within the same variant. Below, we briefly summarise the specific role of algorithmic management according to the three variants of gig work identified in Chapter 2.

App-work

With a focus on the completion of work in local markets, typically with clearly defined labour processes, we suggest that app-work features the most prevalent and advanced algorithmic management processes in the gig economy. A key feature of app-work is the automatic coordination and matching of transactions through a set of advanced algorithms, creating a space where supply and demand integrate through automatic management and enforced mechanisms (Lehdonvirta, 2018). In other words, platforms use algorithms to match supply and demand in the market while also mediating and closely managing the work performed (Newlands, 2020). They enable platforms to track movements and assign tasks using workers' smartphone-based GPS systems. If demand is high at a particular time, the platform organisation may rely on economic "nudges" (Rosenblat & Stark, 2016) in the form of algorithmically determined surge-pricing (Gandini, 2018) – called "boosts" – to entice workers to areas of high demand, a process Woodcock and Johnson (2018) term "gamification-from-above."

Moreover, algorithms are used to undertake typical people management processes like work assignment and performance management without the need for face-to-face interaction (Duggan et al., 2020). App-workers are typically managed via tracking mechanisms and customer ratings, thus forming one of the fundamental principles of the gig economy in that most core people management processes (i.e. the assignment of tasks, performance evaluation) are fulfilled by one of the two groups of users, the worker or the customer, through the medium of the app-work platform (Schmidt, 2017). For example, Uber and Lyft drivers are not directly supervised, nor are they required to wear a uniform or display organisational signage in their vehicles. However, these platform organisations have been known to provide drivers with precise instructions on cleanliness of their workspace, how to behave with customers, and guidelines for maintaining proper hygiene (Steinberger, 2018). Likewise, both organisations monitor the quality of work based on anonymous customer ratings. Thus, algorithmic management has an especially central role in the nature of working relationships in this domain which brings both practical and theoretical challenges (Duggan et al., 2021).

Crowdwork

Algorithmic management processes manifest quite differently in crowdwork. For example, on most platforms, crowdworkers have significant control over choosing which tasks to complete. Depending on the platform organisation's infrastructure, workers may either view a list of tasks that have been posted to the market and search within these, or they may advertise their own services by using keywords to highlight the range of tasks that they are willing to complete for requestors (Keith et al., 2019).

Because crowdwork does not necessarily require the platform organisation to algorithmically link or assign a particular worker to a task or assignment, crowdworkers commonly possess greater autonomy over this particular aspect of their work when compared to many app-workers. However, many crowdwork platforms instead use algorithms to segregate or filter between workers. This may include only allowing workers to access certain tasks based on their location, their percentage of accepted tasks, and the level of experience already gained through tasks previously performed via the platform organisation (Irani, 2014).

Similar to app-work, a key feature of the crowdworker–requester relationship is that worker performance is digitally regulated by an algorithm. Across most crowdwork platforms, requesters' feedback on performance provides a reputation score and may even lead to the rejection of the work, where requesters refuse to pay the worker (Panteli et al., 2020). In such cases, requesters are often not required to explain their actions and there are few dispute resolution systems that workers can draw upon to appeal the decision (Webster, 2016). Consequently, crowdworkers must ensure positive ratings from requesters in order to secure further work – in which case, algorithmic management creates a self-disciplining quality that replaces the need for direct supervision. Workers with the best scores and most experience tended to receive most work due to requesters' preferences and platform organisations' algorithmic ranking of workers within search results (Wood et al., 2019). Interestingly, this type of algorithmic management or control system is operated at the end of the labour process rather than during it, which affords workers the freedom to work however they wish in many cases, provided the end product is accurate and satisfactory to the client (Wood et al., 2019).

However, there are often further hidden but important influences on access to work for crowdworkers. For example, Carr et al. (2017), using an experimental research design of microtask crowdworkers on Fiverr, identified that while the client holds the ultimate hiring decision-making authority the digital platform plays a substantial, albeit subtle, role on this selection. This study indicates that "other information" (e.g. photographs) which although irrelevant to the work task, are part of the platform, can moderate the likelihood of a client contracting an individual or not.

Capital platform work

Compared to app-work and crowdwork, relatively little is known about the specific algorithmic management processes found in capital platform work. However, what is known is that these practices are creating new challenges in capital platform work environments: while some workers use agility and creativity to manipulate algorithmic tools for personal benefit, others are left feeling uncertain and anxious in needing to navigate this new technology in the management of their micro-business (Jarrahi & Sutherland, 2019). Although the labour process is less clearly defined in capital platform work, individuals operating in this domain still have no choice but to be placed in an algorithmic environment. Using the example of Cheng & Foley (2019) discuss the experiences of workers, or hosts, with various aspects of the algorithmic systems embedded on the platform. In particular, they highlight a lack of transparency in the process of ranking and displaying accommodation listings to customers, as well as frustrations and suspicious about the implications for hosts of using the dispute resolution system. Hence, the way the system is set up to operate can create a subtle but powerful means of controlling the practice and behaviours of those engaged in this form of gig work.

Conceptualising algorithmic control in platform organisations

Given the intense variability of the algorithmic control strategies implemented by platform organisations, it is unsurprising that scholarship has struggled with the challenge of fully capturing the intricacies of the mechanisms utilised. In addressing this issue, Kellogg et al. (2020) developed a conceptual framework which seeks to more effectively conceptualise and clarify the nature of algorithmic control in organisations by identifying several broad functions of algorithms in managing and controlling workers' activities. This framework – simply referred to as the "6 Rs of algorithmic control" – draws on established labour process theory to explain the role of algorithms in reconfiguring working relationships. Labour process theory, at its core, seeks to unpack the relationships between employers and workers to understand how this sets in motion the "labour process" (Burawoy, 1979). However, labour process perspectives have historically tended to focus on the traditional, waged workplace, and less so on atypical or informal working arrangements where spatial or temporal dimensions are varied (Thompson & Smith, 2009). Consequently, critics have long argued that this theoretical approach was resistant to acknowledging labour transformations, particularly where non-standard employment forms – such as those found in the gig economy – are concerned (Cappelli & Keller, 2013).

Recent research has argued that labour process theory can be extended beyond its usual territory into the fluid context of the gig economy to study the remediation of social relations in this labour context (Gandini, 2019).

Much of this remediation is brought about by the use of algorithmic tech-nologies, in place of human managers, to enable, monitor, and control inter-actions between parties. Thus, in many ways, a labour process approach to gig work is valuable as it places gig workers and their experiences at the centre of the analysis, allowing researchers to assess labour–capital struggles over the extraction of labour effort (Jaros, 2010; Smith, 2015) – a widely contested issue in the gig economy.

By analysing the role of algorithms as a major force in enabling organi-sations to reconfigure working relations, Kellogg et al.'s (2020) framework integrates knowledge on algorithmic technologies with traditional concep-tualisations of organisational control to examine the notion of "contested terrain" (Edwards, 1979) between organisations and workers. This refers to where managers implement new technologies in efforts to control and max-imise the value created by individuals' labour, while workers, in retaliation, resist and defend their autonomy in the face of tighter employer control. This framework seeks to bridge a notable gap in organisational scholar-ship by regaining pace with the potential of algorithmic technologies to transform organisational control in profound ways and with significant implications for workers. According to Kellogg et al. (2020), algorithms can be used to direct workers by *recommending* and *restricting*, to evaluate workers by *recording* and *rating*, and to discipline workers by *replacing* and *rewarding*.

Algorithmic recommending

The first mechanism used to direct workers refers to the use of algorithms to offer suggestions intended to prompt workers to make decisions preferred by the platform organisation (Kellogg et al., 2020). This can augment work-ers' decisions by automatically finding patterns in the data and prescrib-ing actions based on this, such as recommending specific courses of action and bypassing the heuristics typically used by individuals to make deci-sions. In many cases, these recommendations come in the form of "nudges" that are built into algorithmic systems, often making it difficult for work-ers to ignore. App-work platform Uber is particularly well-known for such prompts by engaging in individualised and real-time nudging by, for exam-ple, actively encouraging drivers to follow particular routes or compelling them to take rest breaks if the algorithm detects erratic driving styles via the application's in-built GPS tracking software (Rosenblat & Stark, 2016). From the perspective of workers, a significant issue to emerge from this is that algorithmic recommending may prosper a feeling of "bosslessness" amongst workers, who operate under the illusion of not having a boss, while still being instructed, guided, and "nudged" by these technological mechanisms (Wu et al., 2019).

Similarly, Kellogg et al. (2020) address further negative outcomes of algorithmic recommending, particularly where "nudges" may not be intelligible to workers or where prompts may not be easily opted out of. Ivanova et al. (2018) note that where workers are afforded choice between different paths of action, platform organisations typically retain control over the way these options are presented. In this way, nudges and prompts are specifically chosen to guide worker behaviour that favour the firm, and unwanted or impermissible alternatives are simply removed from its design (Aneesh, 2009).

Algorithmic restricting

This mechanism, also used to direct workers, refers to the use of algorithms to display only certain information and to allow specific behaviours while preventing others (Kellogg et al., 2020). Interestingly, the role of algorithms in this scenario allows the restriction of information to be incorporated instantaneously and covertly into the work process. For example, particularly in app-work, algorithmic mechanisms embedded on platform organisations may narrow task choices or limit certain details and information about tasks until after the worker has agreed to complete the gig (Gandini, 2018). Likewise, in both crowdwork and capital platform work, evidence suggests that workers lack full information or transparency over a variety of issues related to the assignment of tasks, the monitoring of performance, and the listing of services (Cheng & Foley, 2019; Irani, 2014). Thus, a notable criticism of algorithmic restricting is that it results in feelings of alienation for workers by depriving them of complete control and know-how over their activities. For example, by withholding information on passenger journey details until after the task has been accepted, rideshare workers were often unable to determine how profitable a trip would be until after they had agreed to complete the job (Rosenblat & Stark, 2016). This strategy is likely used to influence workers' decision-making (Shapiro, 2017) and to ensure smooth service offerings for customers. However, there may be greater and more damaging implications for workers in terms of reduced earning potential and diminished autonomy over the labour process.

Algorithmic recording

Used to evaluate workers, this process involves the use of technological procedures to monitor, aggregate, and report a wide variety of finely grained data from internal and external sources (Kellogg et al., 2020). These procedures often occur instantaneously in real time. This data is then used to quantify, compare, and evaluate worker outputs regarding the performance of work tasks (Meijerink & Keegan, 2019). Consequently, there is typically a significant information asymmetry between the information possessed by workers and platforms, related directly to new methods of surveillance and data-gathering enabled by technology (Duggan et al., 2020). This data is then relayed back to workers, via computational procedures, in the form of real-time feedback. Algorithmic recording is extensively used in gig work, and particularly in app-work, where worker performance is continuously monitored via metrics and statistics (Meijerink & Keegan, 2019). For workers, algorithmic recording can shape their subjectivity in that individuals come to see themselves in the ways they are defined through surveillance (Kellogg et al., 2020). Additionally, feelings of constant surveillance can also lead workers to police or alter their own behaviour, perhaps in efforts to comply with organisational expectations or to match the behaviour of their peers.

Algorithmic rating

Also used to evaluate workers, this mechanism refers to the role of algorithms in facilitating efforts to guide worker behaviour. This is enabled via the use of computational technologies which gather ratings and rankings in order to calculate some measure of workers' performance (Kellogg et al., 2020). These ratings can be an ongoing aggregation of quantitative and qualitative feedback, from both internal and external sources (Wood & Lehdonvirta, 2019). Algorithmic rating holds several important consequences for workers, which may be related to potentially discriminatory outcomes based on gender and race stereotyping (Schiek & Gideon, 2018). Additionally, as a function, algorithmic rating typically does not hold the customer to account, but instead focuses entirely on the role of workers by offering few mechanisms for contesting unfair evaluations. Thus, for many gig workers, receiving and sustaining positive ratings is crucially important, with even a small variation in an individual's overall, aggregated score being potentially detrimental for continuity in their role (Birgillito & Birgillito, 2018).

Algorithmic replacing

In disciplining workers, algorithmic replacing may be used to allow platform organisations to rapidly or automatically deactivate (i.e. terminate) underperforming workers, and to replace them with substitute workers. Across most types of gig work, the independent contractor classification allows platform organisations to automatically remove workers from their service if performance metrics or ratings drop below a certain level (Kuhn & Maleki, 2017). The fragmented nature of gig work enables this, where large-scale recruitment can be done with relative speed and ease, meaning a reserve army of workers can be quickly drawn upon to assume the roles of those the organisation, via its algorithms, decides who to replace. Because platform organisations treat workers interchangeably, the loss of those who do not meet or accept the platform's terms is more sustainable and less consequential (Duggan et al., 2020). On the other hand, such strategies are unlikely to impact positively on worker morale, with outcomes instead being likely to include increased feelings of worthlessness and disposability amongst workers. This may also lead to the reduced attraction of gig work to those who may consider it as an option but who have not yet been indoctrinated by the lived experience of the work. These feelings have been reported in an increasing number of studies in this domain (Sherman & Morley, 2020), raising questions about the implications and long-term sustainability of these work practices in the gig economy.

Algorithmic rewarding

This final mechanism, also used to discipline worker behaviour, involves using algorithms to interactively and dynamically reward high-performing workers with more opportunities, higher pay, and promotions (Kellogg et al., 2020). Algorithmic rewarding systems can provide returns in real time for behaviours that comply with predefined guidance, with both professional and material incentives being used to achieve such compliance. For example, cases have been reported of gig workers who complied with assignments or guidance being immediately rewarded with more work, higher pay, and increased flexibility (Kellogg et al., 2020). Thus, in this way, algorithmic rewarding can be used to enhance the availability of greater autonomy and flexibility in scheduling for workers – one of the key selling points of the gig economy. However, as with many algorithmic processes in this domain, the reward systems in use often lack transparency for workers. This can lead to suspicion and frustration around the intentional secrecy of these systems, as well as the opaque and unclear guidelines for accessing and being paid for work (Goods et al., 2019). Although this secrecy seems to be upheld by platform organisations to discourage attempts at manipulation and ratings inflation, such practices create an additional obstacle for workers in navigating the complex labour that they find themselves immersed in.

Conclusion

This chapter has examined the role of technology in shaping and facilitating gig work, with a particular focus on the challenges and opportunities created by the use of algorithmic technologies in monitoring, managing, and controlling the activities of gig workers. In doing so, we first considered the increasing digitalisation of working activities in order to effectively understand the environment from which the gig economy has emerged and prospered. As managerial practices and organisational control strategies continue to be heavily impacted by automation, it seems obvious that the implications – both for workers and organisations – will be substantial. In many cases, this automation is transforming organisations in a way that makes workers less necessary (Gramano, 2019). Yet, our understanding of the specific details and functions of these technologies, as well as the impact on worker experiences, remains significantly underdeveloped.

With this in mind, we turned our attention to enhancing understanding of the nature of the algorithmic technologies found in gig work. We placed a particular focus on the algorithmic technologies used to coordinate and monitor the activities of gig workers. In the literature, the pervasiveness of algorithmic management within different types of platform organisations is receiving increasing attention, often in efforts to decipher how these mechanisms impact on the autonomy of workers (Duggan et al., 2020; Wood et al., 2019). However, across different types of gig work, it quickly becomes apparent that the scope and breadth of algorithmic management processes are incredibly diverse, often differing across variants of gig work and between platform organisations within the same variant (Hyers & Kovacova, 2018). In addressing this challenge, recent research has made efforts to conceptualise the management and control features of algorithms in a more succinct and accessible way (Kellogg et al., 2020), which represents an important starting point in fully identifying and addressing the disruptive role of technology in the gig economy.

References

Aneesh, A. (2009). Global labor: Algocratic modes of organization. *Sociological Theory*, 27 (4): 347–370.

Aroles, J., Mitev, N., & de Vaujany, F.X. (2019). Mapping themes in the study of new work practices. *New Technology, Work and Employment*, 34 (3): 285–299.

Barley, S.R., Bechky, B.A., & Milliken, F.J. (2017). The changing nature of work: Careers, identities, and work lives in the 21st century. *Academy of Management Discoveries*, 3 (2): 111–115.

Birgillito, G., & Birgillito, M. (2018). Algorithms and ratings: Tools to manage labour relations – proposals to renegotiate labour conditions for platform drivers. *Labour & Law Issues*, 4 (2): 26–50.

Burawoy, M. (1979). *Manufacturing Consent: Changes in the Labor Process Under Capitalism.* Chicago, IL: University of Chicago Press.

Cappelli, P., & Keller, J.R. (2013). Classifying work in the new economy. *Academy of Management Review*, 38 (4): 575–596.

Carey, D., & Smith, M. (2016). How companies are using simulations, competitions, and analytics to hire. *Harvard Business Review.* https://hbr.org/2016/04/how-companies-are-using-simulations-competitions-and-analytics-to-hire.

Carr, C.T., Hall, R.D., Mason, A.J., & Varney, E.J. (2017). Cueing employability in the gig economy: Effects of task-relevant and task-irrelevant information on Fiverr. *Management Communication Quarterly*, 31 (3): 409–428.

Cheng, M., & Foley, C. (2019). Algorithmic management: The case of Airbnb. *International Journal of Hospitality Management*, 83: 33–36.

Collier, R.B., Dubal, V.B., & Carter, C. (2017). Labour platforms and gig work: The failure to regulate. *Institute for Research on Labour and Employment: Working Paper 106-17.*

De Stefano, V. (2016). The rise of the "just-in-time" workforce: On-demand work, crowdwork and labour protection in the gig economy. *International Labour Office: Conditions of Work and Employment Series*, 71.

Duggan, J., Sherman, U., Carbery, R., & McDonnell, A. (2020). Algorithmic management and app-work in the gig economy: A research agenda for employment relations and HRM. *Human Resource Management Journal*, 30 (1): 114–132.

Duggan, J., Sherman, U., Carbery, R., & McDonnell, A. (2021). Multi-party working relationships in gig work: Towards a new perspective. In V. Daskalova, G. Jansen, & J. Meijerink (Eds.), *Platform Economy Puzzles: A Multidisciplinary Perspective on Gig Work.* Edward Elgar, 162–186.

Edwards, R. (1979). *Contested Terrain: The Transformation of the Workplace in the Twentieth Century.* Basic Books, New York.

Eurofound (2018). *Automation, Digitalisation and Platforms: Implications for Work and Employment*, Publications Office of the European Union, Luxembourg.

Frost, J. (2017). Uber and the gig economy: Can the legal world keep up? *American Bar Association: The SciTech Lawyer*, 13 (2): 4–7.

Gandini, A. (2018). Labour Process Theory and the Gig Economy. *Human Relations*, 72 (6): 1039–1056.

Gerber, C., & Krzywdzinski, M. (2019). Brave new digital work? New forms of performance control in crowdwork. In S.P. Vallas & A. Kovalainen (Eds.), *Work and Labor in the Digital Age (Research in the Sociology of Work, 33)*, 121–143. Emerald Publishing, Bingley.

Gilbert, C., De Winne, S., & Sels, L. (2011). The influence of line managers and HR department on employees' affective commitment. *International Journal of Human Resource Management*, 22 (8): 1618–1637.

Goods, C., Veen, A., & Barratt, T. (2019). "Is your gig any good?" Analysing job quality in the Australian platform-based food-delivery sector. *Journal of Industrial Relations*, 61 (4): 502–527.

Graham, M., Hjorth, I., & Lehdonvirta, V. (2017). Digital labour and development: Impacts of global digital labour platforms and the gig economy on worker livelihoods. *Transfer: European Review of Labour and Research*, 23 (2): 135–162.

Gramano, E. (2019). Digitalisation and work: Challenges from the platform economy. *Contemporary Social Science*, 15 (4): 476–488.

Griesbach, K., Reich, A., Elliott-Negri, L., & Milkman, R. (2019). Algorithmic control in platform food-delivery work. *Socius: Sociological Research for a Dynamic World*, 5: 1–15.

Hall, R. (2010). Renewing and revising the engagement between labour process theory and technology. In P. Thompson & C. Smith (Eds.), *Working Life: Renewing Labour Process Analysis*, 159–181. Palgrave Macmillan, New York.

Harris, S.D., & Krueger, A.B. (2015). *A Proposal for Modernising Labour Laws for Twenty-First-Century Work: The "Independent Worker."* The Hamilton Project.

Healy, J., Nicholson, D., & Pekarek, A. (2017). Should we take the gig economy seriously? *Labour and Industry: A Journal of the Social and Economic Relations of Work*, 27 (3): 232–248.

Hyers, D., & Kovacova, M. (2018). The economics of the online gig economy: Algorithmic hiring practices, digital labour-market intermediation, and rights for platform workers. *Psychological Issues in Human Resource Management*, 6 (1): 160–165.

Irani, L. (2014). The cultural work of microwork. *New Media & Society*, 17 (5): 720–739.

Ivanova, M., Bronowicka, J., Kocher, E., & Degner, A. (2018). *The App as a Boss? Control and Autonomy in Application-Based Management*. European University Viadrina Frankfurt (Oder). Frankfurt, Germany.

Jabagi, N., Croteau, A.M., Audebrand, L.K., & Marsan, J. (2019). Gig workers' motivation: Thinking beyond carrots and sticks. *Journal of Managerial Psychology*, 34 (4): 192–213.

Jago, A.S. (2019). Algorithms and authenticity. *Academy of Management Discoveries*, 5 (1): 38–56.

Jaros, S. (2010). The core theory: Critiques, defences and advances. In: P. Thompson & C. Smith (Eds.), *Working Life: Renewing Labour Process Analysis*, 70–90. Palgrave, London.

Jarrahi, M.H., & Sutherland, W. (2019). Algorithmic management and algorithmic competencies: Understanding and appropriating algorithms in gig work. In: N. Taylor, C. Christian-Lamb, M. Martin, & B. Nardi (Eds.), *Information in Contemporary Society: Lecture Notes in Computer Science*. Springer, Washington DC, USA. 578–589.

Jarrahi, M.H., Sutherland, W., Nelson, S.B., & Sawyer, S. (2020). Platformic management, boundary resources for gig work, and worker autonomy. *Computer Supported Cooperative Work*, 29: 153–189.

Kalleberg, A.L., & Vallas, S.P. (2018). Probing precarious work: Theory, research, and politics. *Precarious Work: Research in the Sociology of Work*, 31: 1–30.

Keith, M.G., Harms, P., & Tay, L. (2019). Mechanical Turk and the gig economy: Exploring differences between gig workers. *Journal of Managerial Psychology*, 34 (4): 286–306.

Kellogg, K.C., Valentine, M.A., & Christin, A. (2020). Algorithms at work: The new contested terrain of control. *Academy of Management Annals*, 14 (1): 366–410.

Kenney, M., & Zysman, J. (2016). The rise of the platform economy. *Issues in Science and Technology*, 32 (3): 61–69.

Kim, S., Marquis, E., Alahmad, R., Pierce, C.S., & Robert, L.P. (2018). The impacts of platform quality on gig workers' autonomy and job satisfaction. *CSCW Companion*, 3–7 November.

Kuhn, K.M., & Maleki, A. (2017). Micro-entrepreneurs, dependent contractors, and instaserfs: Understanding online labour platform workforces. *Academy of Management Perspectives*, 31 (3): 183–200.

Lee, M.K., Kusbit, D., Metsky, E., & Dabbish, L. (2015). Working with machines: The impact of algorithmic and data-driven management on human workers. *Association for Computing Machinery: Conference on Human Factors in Computing Systems*, 1603–1612.

Lehdonvirta, V. (2018). Flexibility in the gig economy: Managing time on three online piecework platforms. *New Technology, Work and Employment*, 33 (1): 13–29.

Mann, G., & O'Neil, C. (2016). Hiring algorithms are not neutral. *Harvard Business Review*.

Maselli, I., Lenaerts, K., & Beblavy, M. (2016). Five things we need to know about the on-demand economy. *Centre for European Policy Studies*, 21: 1–10.

McGaughey, E. (2018). Taylorooism: When network technology meets corporate power. *Industrial Relations Journal*, 49 (5–6): 459–472.

McIntyre, D., Srinivasan, A., Afuah, A., Gawer, A., & Kretschmer, T. (2020). Multi-sided platforms as new organizational forms. *Academy of Management Perspectives*, in press.

McKinsey (2020). *How Covid-19 Has Pushed Companies over the Technology Tipping Point – and Transformed Business Forever*. McKinsey & Company, 5 October.

Meijerink, J., & Keegan, A. (2019). Conceptualizing human resource management in the gig economy: Toward a platform ecosystem perspective. *Journal of Managerial Psychology*, 34 (4): 214–232.

Meijerink, J., Keegan, A., & Bondarouk, T. (2021). Having their cake and eating it too? Online labour platforms and human resource management as a case of institutional complexity. *International Journal of Human Resource Management*, in press.

Murray, A., Rhymer, J., & Sirmon, D.G. (2020). Humans and technology: Forms of conjoined agency in organizations. *Academy of Management Review*, in press.

Newlands, G. (2020). Algorithmic surveillance in the gig economy: The organisation of work through Lefebvrian conceived space. *Organization Studies*, in press.

Norlander, P., Jukic, N., Varma, A., & Nestorov, S. (2021). The effects of technological supervision on gig workers: Organisational control and motivation of Uber, taxi and limousine drivers. *International Journal of Human Resource Management*, in press.

Ovide, S. (2019). *It's the First Day of the Rest of Lyft's Life*. Bloomberg.

Panteli, N., Rapti, A., & Scholarios, D. (2020). "If he just knew who we were": Microworkers' emerging bonds of attachment in a fragmented employment relationship. *Work, Employment and Society*, 34 (3): 476–494.

Rosenblat, A. (2018). *Uberland: How Algorithms Are Rewriting the Rules of Work.* University of California Press, Oakland.

Rosenblat, A., & Stark, L. (2016). Algorithmic labour and information asymmetries: A case study of Uber's drivers. *International Journal of Communications*, 10 (27): 3758–3784.

Rozzi, F. (2018). The impact of the gig economy on US labour markets: Understanding the role of non-employer firms using econometric models and the example of Uber. *Junior Management Science*, 3 (2): 33–56.

Schafheitle, S., Weibel, A., Ebert, I., Kasper, G., Schank, C., & Leicht-Deobald, U. (2020). No stone left unturned? Towards a framework for the impact of datafication technologies on organizational control. *Academy of Management Discoveries*, 6 (3): 455–487.

Schiek, D., & Gideon, A. (2018). Outsmarting the gig economy through collective bargaining – EU competition law as a barrier to smart cities. *International Review of Law, Computers & Technology*, 32 (2–3): 275–294.

Schmidt, F.A. (2017). *Digital Labour Markets in the Platform Economy: Mapping the Political Challenges of Crowd Work and Gig Work.* Friedrich-Ebert-Stiftung.

Shanahan, G., & Smith, M. (2021). Fair's fair: Psychological contracts and power in platform work. *International Journal of Human Resource Management*, in press.

Shapiro, A. (2017). Between autonomy and control: Strategies of arbitrage in the on-demand economy. *New Media & Society*, 20 (8): 2954–2971.

Sherman, U.P., & Morley, M.J. (2020). What do we measure and how do we elicit it? The use of repertory grid technique in multi-party psychological contract research. *European Journal of Work and Organizational Psychology*, 29 (2): 230–242.

Slee, T. (2017). *What's Yours Is Mine: Against the Sharing Economy.* Scribe, London.

Smith, C. (2015). Continuity and change in labor process analysis forty years after labor and monopoly capital. *Labor Studies Journal*, 40 (3): 222–242.

Steinberger, B.Z. (2018). Redefining employee in the gig economy: Shielding workers from the Uber model. *Fordham Journal of Corporate & Financial Law*, 23: 577–596.

Thompson, P., & Smith, C. (2009). Labour power and labour process: Contesting the marginality of the sociology of work. *Sociology*, 43 (5): 913–930.

Tran, M., & Sokas, R.K. (2017). The gig economy and contingent work: An occupational health assessment. *Journal of Occupational and Environmental Medicine*, 59 (4): 63–66.

Vandaele, K. (2018). *Will Trade Unions Survive in the Platform Economy? Emerging Patterns of Platform Workers' Collective Voice and Representation in Europe.* Working Paper, European Trade Union Institute.

van Doorn, N. (2017). Platform labour: On the gendered and racialised exploitation of low-income service work in the "on-demand" economy. *Information, Communication & Society*, 20 (6): 898–914.

Veen, A., Barratt, T., & Goods, C. (2020). Platform-capital's app-etite for control: A labour process analysis of food-delivery work in Australia. *Work, Employment and Society*, 34 (3): 388–406.

Wang, B., Liu, Y., & Parker, S.K. (2020). How does the use of information communication technology affect individuals: A work design perspective. *Academy of Management Annals*, 14 (2): 695–725.

Webster, J. (2016). Microworkers of the gig economy: Separate and precarious. *New Labor Forum*, 25 (3): 56–64.

Wilburn, K.M., & Wilburn, H.R. (2018). The impact of technology on business and society. *Global Journal of World Business*, 12 (1): 23–39.

Williams, P., McDonald, P., & Mayes, R. (2021). Recruitment in the gig economy: Attraction and selection on digital platforms, *International Journal of Human Resource Management*, doi:10.1080/09585192.2020.1867613

Wood, A.J., & Lehdonvirta, V. (2019). *Platform Labour and Structured Antagonism: Understanding the Origins of Protest in the Gig Economy*. Paper presented at the Oxford Internet Institute Platform Economy Seminar Series, 5 March.

Wood, A.J., Graham, M., Lehdonvirta, V., & Hjorth, I. (2019). Good gig, bad gig: Autonomy and algorithmic control in the global gig economy. *Work, Employment and Society*, 33 (1): 56–75.

Woodcock, J., & Johnson, M.R. (2018). Gamification: What it is, and how to fight it. *The Sociological Review*, 66 (3): 542–558.

Wu, Q., Zhang, H., Li, Z., & Liu, K. (2019). Labor control in the gig economy: Evidence from Uber in China. *Journal of Industrial Relations*, 61 (4): 574–596.

4 Multi-party working relationships

Understanding the experiences of gig workers

Introduction

The continued rise of the gig economy holds significant implications for conceptualisations of work and employment. In turn, there has been extensive scholarly attention in recent years, exploring a wide range of issues such as debates on potential worker misclassification (Cappelli & Keller, 2013; Collier et al., 2017), the role and prevalence of algorithmic technologies (Duggan et al., 2020; Rosenblat, 2018), and concerns relating to organisational control or surveillance in gig work (Newlands, 2020; Schafheitle et al., 2020). While these, and other lines of enquiry, have provided insight into important aspects of gig work, understanding the lived experiences of gig workers forms another important stand of research within this domain. Research on gig workers' experiences has been dynamic in its focus, constantly striving to more fully understand the motivations, opportunities, and struggles encountered by different types of gig workers who engage with various platform organisations (Jabagi et al., 2019; Goods et al., 2019). Yet, given the fluidity and diversity that characterises gig work and gig workers, coupled with the fact that research in this space is still in its relative infancy, it is perhaps unsurprising that a comprehensive understanding of the lived experiences of workers in the gig economy remains elusive.

In this chapter, we synthesise existing research to examine the current state of knowledge on the lived experiences of gig workers. To do this, we first consider the disruptive nature of gig work in creating a complex, digitalised, multi-party working relationship wherein the gig worker – at the very centre of the arrangement – often holds the least power. By considering the role and influence of each party in this unique working relationship, we subsequently develop a greater understanding of the employment relations outcomes in the context of information and power asymmetries. Building on this, we then proceed to examine a number of key labour issues as experienced by gig workers. For example, we discuss research findings

DOI: 10.4324/9780429351488-4

which challenge claims of the supposed autonomy afforded to gig workers, particularly where this may lead to unmet expectations or the potential exploitation of workers (Pichault & McKeown, 2019; Shapiro, 2018).
Additionally, we outline career-related issues in gig work, with a particular
focus on the perspective of gig workers being able to progress or develop a
career based on the experience gained while working with digital platform
organisations (Kost et al., 2020).

Key chapter takeaways

- The fluid, fragmented nature of gig-working arrangements is disruptive
  to traditional understanding of work, conventional employment, and
  the inherent norm of reciprocity.
- A complex, digitalised, multi-party working relationship exists in
  gig work, wherein the gig worker is typically required to meet the
  service demands of customers, as prescribed by the digital platform
  organisation.
- Research broadly indicates that gig workers perceive less autonomy
  over their roles than promised, or that the autonomy granted only
  relates to minute aspects of the work.
- Gig workers are afforded minimal training and development opportunities in their roles, thereby representing a potentially significant risk for
  those engaged in the gig economy on a full-time or long-term basis.

The disruption created by gig work

Across various contexts, literature has identified the value of understanding
workers' perceptions and motivations regarding their employment and the
subsequent impact on productivity, engagement, and willingness to adapt to
change within organisations (Bajwa et al., 2018; Bryant, 2006; Canibano,
2019). However, the breadth of work, workers, and working arrangements
means that the process of gaining such an intricate understanding is far from
straightforward. For example, decades of research on work and employment illustrate the range of differences that exist for individuals who work
as employees for an organisation, versus those who partner with organisations to complete work which has been contracted out (Brown & Medoff,
1989; Weil, 2017). Beyond the obviously contrasting employment classifications assigned to each, scholarship has also emphasised the significant
implications for workers who are excluded from the official workforce: for
example, these individuals tend to earn less than employees completing

identical kinds of work, while also experiencing reduced access to benefits, on-the-job training, and pathways to upward advancement (Weil, 2017).

The rapid growth of the gig economy further accentuates the importance of understanding gig workers' experiences while also making this task all the more difficult. The sourcing of labour via digital platform organisations that intermediate between an invisible, dispersed crowd of workers and those who request their services represents a largely reimagined type of working arrangement (Katz & Krueger, 2019; Meijerink & Keegan, 2019). Ostensibly, we imagine this working relationship as being highly commodified and economic in nature, with a transactional approach to the speedy completion of tasks for piece-rate compensation. As discussed in Chapter 2, this is largely due to the reliance on digital, on-demand features within gig work that facilitate the execution of labour. The very nature of platform organisations, and a critical distinguishing factor of the gig-working relationship, is that these organisations represent a new way of *digitally* organising work and offering services.

While no legal employment relationship exists between the gig worker and digital platform organisation (although this is increasingly being challenged through the courts in several jurisdictions), we instead observe the formation of a complex, multi-party working relationship (see Duggan et al., 2020). In other words, platform organisations function as online businesses that digitally facilitate commercial interactions between at least two parties: workers and customers (Gramano, 2019). Therefore, it is the digital platform organisation that enables the "meeting" between the gig worker and customer, and, in doing so, mediates this relationship (Gandini, 2018). Specifically, in the "app-work" variant of gig work, the scenario is similar: work activities in local markets are conducted through smartphone applications (or "apps"), and managed by intermediary digital platform organisations that intervene in setting minimum quality standards of service and in the selection and management of individuals who perform the work. These management activities and practices are primarily implemented via algorithms – in other words, algorithmic management (see Chapter 3). Thus, this dynamic and alternative exchange agreement likely creates several interdependencies and power dynamics between parties.

In gig work, the algorithmic mechanisms embedded on platform organisations essentially function as a rudimentary management function, holding responsibility for coordinating the working arrangement and implementing activities such as workforce planning, performance management, and job design (Kuhn & Maleki, 2017). While issues relating to the management and upholding of the working relationship lie at the heart of research on work and employment, the very nature of gig work contests established thought by utilising algorithms in place of human managers for executing managerial activities (Meijerink & Keegan, 2019). Thus, gig work poses significant challenges for the conceptualisation and practice of management. Likewise, because gig work is hugely individualised across platforms, identifying and addressing the most challenging implications from the perspective of workers is extremely complex.

The digitalised, multi-party working relationship

The emergence of gig work challenges our most basic understanding of the employment relationship (Meijerink & Keegan, 2019; Taylor et al., 2017). With the increasingly central role of technology and the independent contractor status assigned to gig workers, the traditional concept of a legal employment relationship between an employer and employee is not applicable in this context. The very basis of the gig economy is instead established by platform organisations supplying branded service offerings to customers, without actually employing the providers of these services or owning the assets used in the service provision (Sundararajan, 2014). As a result, most gig workers are unlikely to ever actually meet their "boss" (Barley et al., 2017), but instead operate in a scenario where they serve multiple parties: the platform organisation, the customer, and potentially third-party suppliers such as restaurants that partner with food-delivery platform organisations to provide their services.

Various interdependencies exist between the gig worker and the other parties in the working arrangement, thereby forming a complex working relationship where the worker often holds severely limited power (Duggan et al., 2020). From the platform organisation's perspective, advanced algorithms manage and control exchanges on platforms, ranging from the assignment of tasks, to price-setting, to performance management following the completion of tasks (van Doorn, 2017). Customers also hold a significant role in the working relationship by generating service demand in the first instance, but also in a more crucial capacity by anonymously issuing performance ratings to individual workers (Meijerink & Keegan, 2019). Third-party suppliers, although not present in all gig-working relationships, naturally exert significant influence when they are involved due to the requirement for workers to directly engage with the supplier in order to efficiently and effectively deliver the services offered (Duggan et al., 2021). Accordingly, rather than simply partnering with platform organisations to offer services, most gig workers are at the mercy of digital intermediaries, algorithmic mechanisms, and end-user customers.

Consequently, making sense of the multi-party working relationship that exists in gig work is a complex task. This is primarily because existing legal architecture, seemingly outdated in addressing the unique digital infrastructures and multiple parties found in the gig economy, has not yet gained pace with these transformations (Adams et al., 2018; Xiao, 2019). While some progress is being made in various countries around the world, for the most part, standard employment definitions within existing regulation and provisions typically exclude those engaged in gig-working arrangements (Forde et al., 2017). An obvious starting point in exploring these multi-party relationships is to simply focus on the specific role of each individual party in the gig-working relationship, thereby assessing the dynamics between each party to identify where challenges or struggles emerge. From here, in efforts to more effectively conceptualise this working relationship, researchers have also adopted various theoretical frameworks which allow for the development of insights into this novel arrangement. For example, Meijerink and Keegan (2019) adopt an eco-system perspective to make sense of how gig-working arrangements move beyond the dyadic employer–employee relationship by focusing on the multilateral exchange relationships between the parties involved – and subsequently, the need to govern these exchange relationships in order to co-create value.

Likewise, Duggan et al. (2021) and Shanahan and Smith (2021) both adopt a psychological contract perspective to help in developing a more cohesive understanding of the individualised nature of gig-working relationships, particularly in the absence of a robust legal foundation to the work itself. Differing from the legal contract of employment, psychological contract theory instead examines the mutual, promise-based expectations that parties have of one another and how these implicit expectations impact behaviour (Makin et al., 1996; Rousseau, 1995). While psychological contract theory has traditionally been used to help explain the bilateral working agreement between employees and organisations (Rousseau, 1995), contemporary research has called for a "multi-foci" perspective to better understand the modern workplace, where dependencies exist across multiple parties (Alcover et al., 2017). For example, Sherman and Morley (2020) suggest that for gig workers, the psychological contract held with one party may impinge on the contract created with another party, resulting in complications that arise owing to multiple dependence. This is a significant issue in multi-party working arrangements as there may be consequences for other parties if an individual has depleted resources in trying to fulfil an obligation for one particular party (Deng et al., 2018; Sherman & Morley, 2020). Additionally, the nature of multi-party working relationships may mean that breach of the psychological contract with one party can be triggered by the relationship with another, and perhaps, that the fulfilment of one agreement may come at the expense of another (Wiechers et al., 2019).

These examples illustrate the complexities at the heart of multi-party working arrangements, and raise questions about how these relationships can be effectively managed.

At this point in research on gig-working, building knowledge on the process through which individuals establish a working relationship and how the labour arrangement functions can help us to understand how gig workers are likely to behave and interact with the other parties in the exchange. With multiple, unique sources of dependence across at least three parties, gig work constitutes a working relationship in which platform organisations and customers simultaneously generate dependence and determine the rules that shape, afford, and limit worker agency (Wood & Lehdonvirta, 2019). The concept of agency suggests that individuals express independence through self-assertion and control over environments, work processes, or outcomes (Marshall, 1989). We now consider the role of each party in the working arrangement – the gig worker, the platform organisation, and the customer – to build understanding and unpack the multi-party relationship that exists in gig work. In doing so, we explore how each party is likely to shape the working relationship for individual gig workers through the formation of various interdependencies and power asymmetries.

The gig worker

Considering gig work is not rooted in traditional employer–employee dyads but rather in polyadic arrangements, it seems likely that agency will be significantly lower for gig workers compared to those in traditional employment (Healy et al., 2017). However, despite this, gig workers are still required to perform synchronous tasks, often for a local, visible client, and remuneration is typically predetermined (Kuhn & Maleki, 2017). Due to this seemingly transparent agentic relationship, it can be argued that those engaged in gig work may still develop a working relationship with the platform organisations for whom they work (Duggan et al., 2021).

Likewise, the involvement of three, or potentially four, parties in certain gig-working arrangements further complicates the relationship for workers. For example, in the case of food-delivery app-work across platforms such as UberEats, Deliveroo, and Foodora, workers are faced with a triangular working arrangement whereby they serve multiple agents: they act on behalf of the *platform organisation*, but also on behalf of the food outlet or *restaurant* for whom they are delivering orders (Cochrane & McKeown, 2015). Likewise, these workers are also the only party with direct engagement with the *customer* who ordered the food, who then can anonymously rate their performance and/or their overall satisfaction with the service. In this way, gig workers may not identify one single "agent" in the working relationship, but instead will perceive themselves to form part of a complex web of multi-dependency derived from multiple actors in the employment network (Duggan et al., 2021).

It also becomes apparent that the typical architecture of the employment relationship, such as negotiation and trust, do not seem to apply in the gig economy (Makoff, 2017). This aligns with recent research suggesting that the realities experienced by many gig workers are significantly different to what was advertised (Harris, 2017, Wood et al., 2019). For example, studies illustrate the dissatisfaction and unmet expectations felt by gig workers in relation to power asymmetries, autonomous working, and compensation levels (Möhlmann & Zalmanson, 2017; Shapiro, 2017). Yet, as the gig worker may perceive different levels of satisfaction from different parties in the working relationship (i.e. perhaps from the platform organisation at one instance and from the restaurant at another), this raises the possibility that the working relationship that exists between each individual and the other parties in the arrangement may differ substantially across gig workers (Wiechers et al., 2019). In other words, it should not be assumed that all gig-working arrangements are homogenous in being entirely economic or transactional, simply because the relationship has been established in some way by the platform organisation. Indeed, evidence is now emerging that some gig workers seek a broader, more co-determined relationship with the other parties (Sherman & Morley, 2020, Ashford et al., 2018)

The platform organisation

The nature and role of platform organisations represents one of the most challenging aspects of gig-working relationships. This is because platform organisations both maintain and distance themselves from responsibility over the markets that they create: on the one hand, they retain control over the allocation of work, conditions, and minimum performance standards; but, on the other, they deny many responsibilities by identifying only as "technological companies" who serve to provide a medium of exchange (Healy et al., 2017). A key feature of gig work is the automatic coordination and matching of the transaction through a set of advanced algorithms, creating a space where supply and demand integrate through automatic management and enforced mechanisms (Lehdonvirta, 2018). In other words, platform organisations use algorithms to match supply and demand in the market while also mediating and closely monitoring the work performed (Gandini, 2019).

As a technology-enabled monitoring tool, algorithmic management eliminates the more interpersonal and empathetic aspects of people management. By automating management practice, algorithms exert control over workforces and facilitate asymmetrical information in the working relationship. Likewise, many platform organisations fully exploit the possibility to minutely monitor the activities of gig workers in real time, rendering them heavily at the mercy of the platform's expectations and demands (Kuhn & Maleki, 2017). This "always-on" form of control is seen as unfair by some gig workers, particularly given their legal employment classification as self-employed, independent contractors rather than employees (Gandini, 2019).

In its role as intermediary, the platform organisation is the only party with full access to and control over the data, processes, and rules of the platform (Jabagi et al., 2019). Yet, as noted by Jago (2019), people believe that technological agents lack the same level of moral authenticity as human agents. This arms-length approach to managing workers, characterised by data-driven performance statistics and metrics, signals towards the development of a heavily economic and transactional working arrangement. However, recent research by Bankins and Formosa (2020) argues that through increasing sophistication, artificially intelligent technologies are now moving away from being viewed as a simple "tool" used by organisations towards being seen as "partners" of and within organisations. Findings like this support the argument that the gig worker, in part at least, may develop more relational expectations of the platform organisation, even if the platform itself rejects this notion (Duggan et al., 2021; Sherman & Morley, 2020).

The customer

The third absolute party in gig-working relationships is the customer or client who requests the services offered by platform organisations. Although ostensibly the most passive party in the working relationship, customers may play an influential role in shaping the gig-working arrangement (Duggan et al., 2021). This is because many platform organisations utilise customer ratings of workers via anonymous systems as a means of performance evaluation. Before being shared with gig workers, assessments are forwarded to platform organisations, who have the opportunity to verify – albeit indirectly – the quality and punctuality of the service rendered (Gramano, 2019). These data, along with customer ratings and reviews, may then be used to identify the best performing workers and to alter the algorithm that assigns tasks to workers. This process is especially commonplace in app-work, wherein workers are subject to tight levels of control and where the customer evaluation is often critical (Healy et al., 2017), often without recourse to questioning or refuting performance scores. In some instances, the rating issued by the customer may not solely reflect the individual worker's performance, but the overall service delivery (e.g. delays from the restaurant). This can potentially be detrimental for workers and arguably results in a generally one-sided process (Flanagan, 2018), which intimates a further shift in power away from the gig worker.

As gig workers are potentially rated after the completion of each individual task, the combined roles of the customer and the platform organisation essentially exercise penetrating control over all aspects of the service delivery (Duggan et al., 2021). In this sense, the gig worker can be described as being in a situation comparable to a permanent probationary period (Gramano, 2019). Yet, given the fundamental role of customer ratings, in that workers in receipt of low ratings are potentially subjected to being deactivated (Tran & Sokas, 2017), concerns are raised around the inherent weaknesses in simplistic and entirely quantitative measures of performance (McDonnell et al., 2019). For example, in some cities, Uber drivers with an average rating, calculated by an algorithm, of lower than 4.6 out of a possible 5 are at risk of disbarment from the platform (Kuhn & Maleki, 2017). Likewise, considering the customer's role, another risk is that gig work is supplied entirely through IT channels, be it online platforms or apps, potentially distorting the perceptions customers may have of these workers and significantly contributing to a perceived dehumanisation of their activities (De Stefano, 2016).

The experiences of gig workers

Having examined the specific role of each party in the gig-working relationship, and importantly, the nature of the engagements that likely occur between each of these parties, we now turn our attention to exploring the various implications of this arrangement. In doing so, we focus exclusively on the perspective of individual gig workers, who operate at the core of the working relationship by completing most major aspects of the labour process, seemingly at the mercy and command of all other parties. In this section, we focus on three particular areas: employment relations issues; gig workers' job autonomy; and career-related matters. While these three areas are not exhaustive in capturing the full experiences of gig workers, we believe that much existing literature in this domain has identified the issues presented below as representing some of the most significant that pertain to this context.

Employment relations issues

The fragmented nature of gig work, through its reliance on technology via digital platforms and governing algorithms, appears likely to erode the reciprocity found in traditional employment relationships. In this way, gig work challenges our understanding of employment relations concepts and practices, with the overall approach differing significantly from established models, both in the context of its strategic purpose and the way in which activities are delivered and implemented (Meijerink et al., 2021). In most ways, gig work seems to pass the risks of employment almost entirely on to individual workers, predicated by the organisational view that these workers are independent, self-employed contractors.

A heavily economic relationship appears to be at the heart of gig work, with individuals paid for the quantity of work undertaken rather than the time spent working. The seemingly non-existent focus on the development of mutual trust and commitment in the working relationship further solidifies the transactional nature of this exchange. At the recruitment stage, most roles are advertised on the basis that workers have the autonomy to work when they wish with considerable independence, indicating that there is little or no expectation of a long-term relationship unless desired (Jabagi et al., 2019). Likewise, workers are typically onboarded quickly, via a prompt screening process, ensuring a readily accessible source of labour for the organisation (Kuhn & Maleki, 2017). While this approach to onboarding workers certainly reduces costs by eliminating many of the labour and time costs involved (Healy et al., 2017), it may prove problematic when looking beyond short-term, transactional cost benefits towards recruiting motivated workers who are likely to succeed in roles.

Thus, on the surface, the denial of employment status for gig workers might suggest that this form of labour is of little relevance for management as a profession and function. However, with multiple court rulings making determinations in favour of individual workers gaining employment status, such issues naturally become increasingly germane. Notwithstanding this, existing literature highlights that managerial practices are indeed implemented for gig workers, despite the lack of an officially defined function. Algorithmic management, as one of the defining features of gig work, significantly impacts on the functioning of the working relationship. For example, several studies have examined the role of algorithms in managing the performance of gig workers (e.g. Prassl, 2018; Rosenblat, 2018; Veen et al., 2020). Performance management is about creating motivation and commitment to achieve organisational objectives (Verweire & Berghe, 2004). Yet, performance management in the gig economy differs substantially from the traditional approach (Barley et al., 2017), by instead focusing primarily on quantitative customer ratings and tracking workers via an algorithm. Although algorithmic management often relies on inputs from customers or requesters, algorithms can contain significant biases (Guszcza et al., 2018), and the platform organisation has little control over the quality of information collected. Thus, without human interpretation, the extensive use of data and algorithms can be problematic, especially as regards performance measures and appraisals, which can rarely be challenged by gig workers (Healy et al., 2017). Thus, gig workers who receive low ratings can be subjected to discrimination on the platform, arbitrarily sanctioned (Prassl, 2018), or even ruled out for future work (Tran & Sokas, 2017). In addition, when low ratings are mentioned, this may be a somewhat inaccurate descriptor as the score received may still equate to what many would consider high performance (Kuhn & Maleki, 2017).

Shared understanding and reciprocal contributions for mutual benefit are at the core of traditional, functional exchange relationships between workers and organisations (Dabos & Rousseau, 2004). From the gig worker's perspective, having no say in how work is assigned and how performance is assessed means that the working relationship is less representative of one that has been mutually co-determined, and could instead be perceived as a working arrangement of subjugation (Harvey et al., 2017). According to organisational support theory, employees interpret organisational policies, practices, and treatment as indicators of the organisation's support and commitment to them (Vanhala & Ritala, 2016). For gig workers, traditional understanding around reciprocity and organisational support no longer applies or, at a minimum, are considerably different. In its role as intermediary, the digital platform organisation is the only party with full access to and control over the data, processes, and rules of the platform (Jabagi et al., 2019) Subsequently, the low levels of control over evaluation processes on the platform and the apparent vulnerability of gig workers can potentially result in voluntary departure from the platform. As reported by the mass media, high employee turnover is becoming a problem for labour platforms, even forcing some to lower their performance expectations and ease some job requirements (McGee, 2017).

Thus, while the gig-working relationship initially appears to be an entirely transactional, economic exchange, recent research on the nuances of gig work signals the potential existence of a more complex, textured scenario, wherein gig workers view, or strive to view, their association with the digital platform organisation in a broader, more relational sense (Ashford et al., 2018). For instance, some gig workers are reported as seeking professional development opportunities from organisations (Graham et al., 2017), social interaction and support from colleagues and managers, and mentoring from more senior colleagues (Ashford et al., 2018).

Job autonomy in gig work

The role of algorithmic management in governing the gig-working relationship creates significant challenges for gig workers' autonomy. Proponents have generally viewed gig workers as part of a newly empowered, flexible workforce that can choose where and when to work, arguing that these arrangements offer opportunities for greater autonomy over the work arrangements offered via digital platform organisations (Healy et al., 2017; Kuhn & Maleki, 2017). Indeed, it is important to recognise that gig workers are granted new and different types of flexibility when compared to conventional employees, with such autonomy primarily associated with individual ability to schedule work at their discretion (Shanahan & Smith, 2021). Others, however, are more critical and argue that gig workers' autonomy is limited due to the influence of platform organisations, who are seen to exercise significant control over the labour process by implementing structural and operational choices that reduce flexibility and encourage economic dependency on the platform organisation (Wood et al., 2019; Veen et al., 2020).

Scholars have generally understood worker autonomy as the ability to exercise control over the content, timing, and performance of activities (Porter & Steers, 1973). Comprising of control, tracking, and surveillance mechanisms, the algorithmic management function is all-encompassing in monitoring the activities of gig workers. Therefore, gig work can be characterised as what Mazmanian, Orlikowski, and Yates (2013) term "the autonomy paradox." Essentially, while afforded flexibility over when to work and which tasks to accept, workers are subjected to new forms of control and surveillance, limiting aspects of their autonomy. Consequently, gig workers are apparently required to adhere to the structures implemented by platforms, operating under a type of "illusionary flexibility" that allows these organisations to retain control over most meaningful elements of the work and to reap maximum benefits from labour (Kellogg et al., 2020; Smith & Leberstein, 2015). However, to date, relatively little is known about gig workers' attitudes or responses to the algorithmic management function, and more specifically, whether workers perceive these mechanisms as impeding their ability to control important aspects of their work.

With a heavy reliance on algorithmic mechanisms, combined with a lack of transparency around how these algorithms work, gig workers face significant sensemaking efforts to become familiar with the management and control processes under which their work is structured (Josserand & Kaine, 2019; Norlander et al., 2021). Likewise, platform organisations' reliance on data requires a level of surveillance that is not present in most workplaces, and which seems likely to create significant information and power asymmetries between the worker and the platform (Bader & Kaiser, 2019; Lepanjuuri et al., 2018). Despite the presentation of the gig-working relationship as a type of partnership between independent workers and platform organisations, research generally points towards the idea that the power dynamics in this relationship are often not bilateral, but rather may rest to a large degree with the platform organisation (Kuhn & Maleki, 2017). For gig workers, the supposed autonomy resulting from algorithmic management processes can lead to overwork, sleep deprivation, and exhaustion as consequences of the "always-on" form of control and the weak structural power of individual workers (Gandini, 2018; Mantymaki et al., 2019).

Career-related issues for gig workers

The issue of developing careers in the gig economy is highly complex. Gig work represents a radical shift from human-centred management within the boundaries of an organisation towards self-management, enabled and remotely monitored by algorithmic technologies (Duggan et al., 2020). These algorithmic technologies, while innovative, create a hyper-flexibility that leaves workers isolated in roles and without secure employment, development opportunities, or a progressive career path (Ashford et al., 2018). In line with this, the concept of a "career" in the gig economy has been debated, with much disagreement on the potential that exists for career progression (Jabagi et al., 2019; Kost et al., 2020). As independent contractors, gig workers should possess high levels of control and autonomy over their work and career choices (Kuhn & Maleki, 2017). In fact, it is likely the attraction of increased autonomy over scheduling and work that reinforces the sentiment that the quality and flexibility of work life is greater outside of traditional work settings (Sutherland et al., 2020). However, the agentic relationship that exists between the platform organisation and gig workers, wherein the organisation digitally mediates work via the algorithmic management function, complicates this (Duggan et al., 2020).

Differing significantly from traditional conceptualisations of careers where workers progress hierarchically in an often-predictable sequence (Clarke, 2013), contemporary careers are more self-directed and focus on the fulfilment of personal values. Such thinking places emphasis on the individual's subjective interpretation of what constitutes a career, focusing less on progression with one employer (Arthur & Rousseau, 1996), and more on the development of a career across industrial and organisational boundaries. These changes have, in turn, brought several new conceptualisations, such as boundaryless, protean, and kaleidoscope careers (Sullivan & Baruch, 2009). The emergence of the gig economy, however, challenges these ideas. Through its seemingly precarious and casual employment opportunities, gig work does not easily align with prosperous, progressive career thinking. Consequently, the ability of gig workers to learn, progress, and develop career opportunities is uncertain. While research on careers in precarious employment is long-established (Zeitz et al., 2009), gig work represents a novel form of insecure working, hinged on complex algorithms and hyper-flexible arrangements.

Ostensibly, gig work appears to align closely with the development of boundaryless careers: arrangements lack hierarchical reporting relationships (Storey et al., 2005), temporal attachment is relatively low (Kuhn & Maleki, 2017), and thresholds are minimal for crossing between or working for multiple platforms (Gherardi & Murgia, 2013). Thus, the potential for gig workers to form anything resembling an "organisational career" (Clarke, 2013) is extremely limited. On the other hand, however, the reality of the gig-working arrangement is vastly different, with organisations tightly managing workforces while withholding benefits and opportunities (Meijerink & Keegan, 2019). Because of this, arrangements are typically characterised by low job security, reduced commitment, and decreased loyalty between parties (Wood et al., 2019). The diminished potential for development raises noteworthy questions about gig workers' perceptions of roles that typically lack sustainability and prosperity, particularly for those seeking to pursue a more progression-based career and relational arrangement with the "organisation" (Kost et al., 2020).

Gig workers' employment status and the overall anonymity of the gig economy renders them as immediately peripheral to the platform organisation. By utilising algorithmic technologies to manage the working relationship, most gig workers are largely dispersed and work in isolation, relying on the organisation's proprietary application for all guidance on processes (Kaine & Josserand, 2019). Consequently, workers have minimal human interaction with management or fellow workers, preventing the development of more traditional working relationships (Duggan et al., 2020). If gig work lacks prosperity, workers must hold an increasingly active role in ensuring their employability to enable them to pursue a career in line with their values (Strauss et al., 2012). Yet, the low-commitment, "arms-length" approach to working relations makes it unclear how gig workers navigate these arrangements. On the other hand, if gig work is deliberately designed to be unsustainable (Duggan et al., 2020), perhaps it is the platform organisation that is ultimately left vulnerable to the ease at which workers can leave. Thus, organisations must seek to retain ample gig workers to remain attractive to clients – a crux that Kost et al. (2020) describe as counter-intuitive, given the gig economy's inherent business model.

Finally, there remains uncertainty over how gig-work experiences contribute to the development of a career once a worker seeks employment opportunities outside of this domain. For instance, what transferable skills or knowledge can be acquired during gig work that can help individuals to further their career in a new industry? Do employers value work experience in the gig economy when assessing a prospective candidate for a new role? What can platform organisations do to help develop career competencies in gig workers, particularly when the platform organisation itself does not view gig work as a long-term career option for its workers? Should there be an expectation placed on these organisations to offer developmental opportunities? Future scholarship addressing these, and other questions regarding gig workers' career mobility once they leave this domain, is needed.

Conclusion

This chapter has examined the implications arising from the unique, multi-party working relationship found in gig work, with a particular focus on the experiences of gig workers in attempting to navigate this complex arrangement. We first considered the disruption created by the gig economy in the spheres of work and employment, by considering how the dynamic nature of gig work is inherently transformative to existing, conventional conceptualisations (Gandini, 2019). From here, we turn to attempting to understand the intricacies of the working relationship found in gig work, where multiple parties are involved, and where digitalisation and algorithmic technologies give rise to complex, novel interdependencies between these parties. We examined the role of each party in the working arrangement – the gig worker, platform organisation, and customer – and attempted to clarify the specific nature of the engagements that occur between these parties.

Having gained a greater understanding of how the gig-working arrangement functions, the second half of this chapter focused exclusively on the lived experiences of gig workers in attempting to navigate the opportunities and challenges encountered in their roles. Specifically, we reflected on the most prominent employment-relations issues in gig work, exploring the speed at which gig workers are onboarded and immersed into this complex arrangement, and the controversial issues associated with the performance monitoring and evaluation tools found in most types of gig work (Bader & Kaiser, 2019; Norlander et al., 2021). We also examined perceptions of job autonomy for gig workers, with a particular focus on juxtaposing the reality of working under the governance of an algorithmic control system versus the promises of flexibility which are often promoted by platform organisations (Kuhn & Maleki, 2017; Mantymaki et al., 2019). Finally, we considered career-related issues for gig workers, where individuals find themselves in heavily precarious roles with minimal opportunities for advancement or skills development (Ashford et al., 2018; Kost et al., 2020). In considering these key issues surrounding the lived experiences of gig workers – from a multitude of disciplinary perspectives – it is important to recognise such scholarship is in its relative infancy.

References

Adams, A., Freedman, J., & Prassl, J. (2018). Rethinking legal taxonomies for the gig economy, *Oxford Review of Economic Policy*, 34 (3): 475–494.

Alcover, C.M., Rico, R., Turnley, W.H. & Bolino, M.C. (2017). Multi-dependence in the formation of the distributed psychological contract. *European Journal of Work and Organisational Psychology*, 26 (1): 16–29.

Arthur, M.B., & Rousseau, D.M. (1996). *The Boundaryless Career*. Oxford University Press, New York.

Ashford, S.J., Caza, B.B., & Reid, E.M. (2018). From surviving to thriving in the gig economy: A research Agenda for individuals in the new world of work. *Research in Organizational Behavior*. 38: 23–41.

Bader, V., & Kaiser, S. (2019). Algorithmic decision-making? The user interface and its role for human involvement in decisions supported by artificial intelligence. *Organization*, 26 (5): 655–672.

Bajwa, U., Knorr, L., Di Ruggiero, E., Gastaldo, D. & Zendel, A. (2018). *Towards an Understanding of Workers' Experiences in the Global Gig Economy*. University of Toronto, Dalla Lana School of Public Health, Toronto.

Bankins, S., & Formosa, P. (2020). When AI meets PC: Exploring the implications of workplace social robots and a human-robot psychological contract. *European Journal of Work and Organizational Psychology*, 29 (2): 215–229.

Bankins, S., Griep, Y., & Hansen, S.D. (2020). Charting directions for a new research era: Addressing gaps and advancing scholarship in the study of psychological contracts. *European Journal of Work and Organizational Psychology*, 29 (2): 159–163.

Barley, S.R., Bechky, B.A., & Milliken, F.J. (2017). The changing nature of work: Careers, identities, and work lives in the 21st century. *Academy of Management Discoveries*, 3 (2): 111–115.

Brown, C. & Medoff, J. (1989). The employer size-wage effect. *Journal of Political Economy*, 97 (5): 1027–1059.

Bryant, M. (2006). Talking about change: Understanding employee responses through qualitative research. *Management Decisions*, 44 (2): 246–258.

Canibano, A. (2019). Workplace flexibility as a paradoxical phenomenon: Exploring employee experiences. *Human Relations*, 72 (2): 444–470.

Cappelli, P., & Keller, J.R. (2013). Classifying work in the new economy. *Academy of Management Review*, 38 (4): 575–596.

Clarke, M. (2013). The organisational career: Not dead but in need of redefinition. *International Journal of Human Resource Management*, 24 (4): 684–703.

Cochrane, R., & McKeown, T. (2015). Vulnerability and agency work: From the workers' perspectives. *International Journal of Manpower*, 36 (6): 947–965.

Collier, R.B., Dubal, V.B., & Carter, C. (2017). Labour platforms and gig work: The failure to regulate. *Institute for Research on Labour and Employment: Working Paper 106-17.*

Dabos, G.E., & Rousseau, D.M. (2004). Mutuality and reciprocity in the psychological contracts of employees and employers. *Journal of Applied Psychology*, 89 (1): 52–72.

De Stefano, V. (2016). The rise of the "just-in-time" workforce: On-demand work, crowdwork and labour protection in the gig economy. *International Labour Office: Conditions of Work and Employment Series*, 71.

Deng, H., Coyle-Shapiro, J., & Yang, Q. (2018). Beyond reciprocity: A conservation of resources view on the effects of psychological contract violation on third parties. *Journal of Applied Psychology*, 103 (5): 561–77.

Duggan, J., Sherman, U., Carbery, R., & McDonnell, A. (2020). Algorithmic management and app-work in the gig economy: A research agenda for employment relations and HRM. *Human Resource Management Journal*, 30 (1): 114–132.

Duggan, J., Sherman, U., Carbery, R., & McDonnell, A. (2021). Multi-party working relationships in gig work: Towards a new perspective. In V. Daskalova, G. Jansen, & J. Meijerink (Eds.), *Platform Economy Puzzles: A Multidisciplinary Perspective on Gig Work*. Edward Elgar, in press.

Flanagan, F. (2018). Theorising the gig economy and home-based service work. *Journal of Industrial Relations*, 61 (1): 57–78.

Forde, C., Stuart, M., Joyce, S., Oliver, L., Valizade, D., Alberti, G., Hardy, K., Trappmann, V., Imney, C., & Carson, C. (2017). The social protection of workers in the platform economy. *Policy Department A: Economic and Scientific Policy*, Brussels, Belgium.

Gandini, A. (2018). Labour process theory and the gig economy. *Human Relations*, 72 (6): 1039–1056.

Gherardi, S., & Murgia, A. (2013). By hook or by crook: Flexible workers between exploration and exploitation. In M. Holmqvist & A. Spicer (Eds.), *Research in the Sociology of Organizations*, 75–103. Emerald, York.

Goods, C., Veen, A., & Barratt, T. (2019). "Is your gig any good?" Analysing job quality in the Australian platform-based food-delivery sector. *Journal of Industrial Relations*, 61 (4): 502–527.

Graham, M., Hjorth, I. & Lehdonvirta, V. (2017). Digital labour and development: Impacts of global digital labour platforms and the gig economy on worker livelihoods. *Transfer: European Review of Labour and Research*, 23 (2): 135–162.

Gramano, E. (2019). Digitalisation and work: Challenges from the platform economy. *Contemporary Social Science*, 15 (4): 476–488.

Guszcza, J., Rahwan, I., Bible, W., Cebrian, M., & Katyal, V. (2018). Why we need to audit algorithms. *Harvard Business Review*.

Harris, B. (2017). Uber, Lyft, and regulating the sharing economy. *Seattle University Law Review*, 41 (1): 269–285.

Harvey, G., Rhodes, C., Vachhani, S.J., & Williams, K. (2017). Neo-Villeiny and the service sector: The case of hyper flexible and precarious work in fitness centres. *Work, Employment and Society*, 31 (1): 19–35.

Healy, J., Nicholson, D., & Pekarek, A. (2017). Should we take the gig economy seriously? *Labour and Industry: A Journal of the Social and Economic Relations of Work*, 27 (3): 232–248.

Jabagi, N., Croteau, A.M., Audebrand, L.K., & Marsan, J. (2019). Gig workers' motivation: Thinking beyond carrots and sticks. *Journal of Managerial Psychology*, 34 (4): 192–213.

Jago, A.S. (2019). Algorithms and authenticity. *Academy of Management Discoveries*, 5 (1): 38–56.

Josserand, E. & Kaine, S. (2019). Different directions or the same route? The varied identities of ride-share drivers. *Journal of Industrial Relations*, 61 (4): 549–573.

Kaine, S. & Josserand, E.(2019). The organisation and experience of work in the gig economy. *Journal of Industrial Relations*, 61 (4): 479–501.

Katz, L.F. & Krueger, A.B. (2019). The rise and nature of alternative work arrangements in the United States, 1995–2015. *ILR Review*, 72 (2): 382–416.

Kellogg, K.C., Valentine, M.A., & Christin, A. (2020). Algorithms at work: The new contested terrain of control. *Academy of Management Annals*, 14 (1): 366–410.

Kost, D., Fieseler, C., & Wong, S.I. (2020). Boundaryless careers in the gig economy: An oxymoron? *Human Resource Management Journal*, 30 (1): 100–113.

Kuhn, K.M. & Maleki, A. (2017). Micro-entrepreneurs, dependent contractors, and instaserfs: Understanding online labour platform workforces. *Academy of Management Perspectives*, 31 (3): 183–200.

Lehdonvirta, V. (2018). Flexibility in the gig economy: Managing time on three online piecework platforms. *New Technology, Work and Employment*, 33 (1): 13–29.

Lepanjuuri, K., Wishart, R. & Cornick, P. (2018). *The Characteristics of Those in the Gig Economy*. Department for Business, Energy & Industrial Strategy, London, UK.

Makin, P.J., Cooper, C.L., & Cox, C.J. (1996). *Organisations and the Psychological Contract: Managing People at Work*. Wiley-Blackwell, Leicester.

Makoff, A. (2017). Nearly eight million people thinking about joining gig economy, study reveals. *CIPD: People Management*, April 27.

Mantymaki, M., Baiyere, A., & Najmul-Islam, A.K.M.(2019). Digital platforms and the changing nature of physical work: Insights from ride-hailing. *International Journal of Information Management*, 49: 452–460.

Marshall, J. (1989). Re-visioning career concepts: A feminist invitation. In M.B. Arthur, D.T. Hall, & B.S. Lawrence (Eds.), *Handbook of Career Theory*, 275–291. Cambridge University Press, New York.

Mazmanian, M., Orlikowski, W.J., & Yates, J. (2013). The autonomy paradox: The implications of mobile email devices for knowledge professionals. *Organization Science*, 24 (5): 1337–1357.

McDonnell, A., Gunnigle, P., & Murphy, K.R. (2019). Performance management. In D.G. Collings, G. Wood, & L. Samosi (Eds), *Human Resource Management: A Critical Approach*. Routledge, London, 201–219.

McGee, C. (2017). Only 4% of uber drivers remain on the platform a year later, says report. *CNBC Technology*, April 20.

Meijerink, J., & Keegan, A. (2019). Conceptualizing human resource management in the gig economy: Toward a platform ecosystem perspective. *Journal of Managerial Psychology*, 34 (4): 214–232.

Meijerink, J., Keegan, A., & Bondarouk, T. (2021). Having their cake and eating it too? Online labour platforms and human resource management as a case of institutional complexity. *International Journal of Human Resource Management*, in press.

Möhlmann, M., & Zalmanson, L. (2017). Hands on the wheel: Navigating algorithmic management and Uber drivers' autonomy. *Proceedings of the International Conference on Information Systems (ICIS)*, Seoul South Korea, 10–13 December.

Newlands, G. (2020). Algorithmic surveillance in the gig economy: The organisation of work through Lefebvrian conceived space. *Organization Studies*, in press.

Norlander, P., Jukic, N., Varma, A., & Nestorov, S. (2021). The effects of technological supervision on gig workers: Organisational control and motivation of Uber, taxi and limousine drivers. *International Journal of Human Resource Management*, in press.

Pichault, F. & McKeown, T. (2019). Autonomy at work in the gig economy: Analysing work status, work content and working conditions of independent professionals. *New Technology, Work and Employment*, 34 (1): 59–72.

Porter, L.W., & Steers, R.M. (1973). Organizational, work, and personal factors in employee turnover and absenteeism. *Psychological Bulletin*, 80 (2): 151–176.

Prassl, J. (2018). *Humans as a Service*. Oxford University Press, Oxford.

Rosenblat, A. (2018). *Uberland: How Algorithms Are Rewriting the Rules of Work*. University of California Press, Oakland.

Rousseau, D.M. (1995). *Psychological Contracts in Organisations: Understanding Written and Unwritten Agreements*. SAGE Publications, London.

Schafheitle, S., Weibel, A., Ebert, I., Kasper, G., Schank, C., & Leicht-Deobald, U. (2020). No stone left unturned? Towards a framework for the impact of datafication technologies on organizational control. *Academy of Management Discoveries*, 6 (3): 455–487.

Shanahan, G., & Smith, M. (2021). Fair's fair: Psychological contracts and power in platform work. *International Journal of Human Resource Management*, in press.

Shapiro, A. (2018). Between autonomy and control: Strategies of arbitrage in the on-demand economy. *New Media & Society*, 20 (8): 2954–2971.

Sherman, U.P., & Morley, M.J. (2020). What do we measure and how do we elicit it? The case for the use of repertory grid techniques in multi-party psychological contract research. *European Journal of Work and Organizational Psychology*, 29 (2): 230–242.

Smith, R. & Leberstein, S. (2015). *Rights on Demand: Ensuring Workplace Standards and Worker Security in the On-Demand Economy*. National Employment Law Project, New York.

Storey, J., Salaman, G., & Platman, K. (2005). Living with enterprise in an enterprise economy: Freelance and contract workers in the media. *Human Relations*, 58 (8): 1033–1054.

Strauss, K., Griffin, M.A., & Parker, S.K.(2012). Future work selves: How salient identities motivate proactive career behaviours. *Journal of Applied Psychology*, 97 (3): 580–598.

Sullivan, S.E., & Baruch, Y. (2009). Advances in career theory and research: A critical review and agenda for future exploration. *Journal of Management*, 35 (6): 1542–1571.

Sundararajan, A. (2014). What Airbnb gets about culture that uber doesn't. *Harvard Business Review*, 27 November.

Sutherland, W., Jarrahi, M.H., Dunn, M., & Nelson, S.B. (2020). Work precarity and gig literacies in online freelancing. *Work, Employment and Society*, 34 (3): 457–475.

Taylor, M., Marsh, G., Nicol, D. and Broadbent, P. (2017). *Good Work: The Taylor Review of Modern Working Practices*. Department of Business, Energy and Industrial, London.

Tran, M., & Sokas, R.K. (2017). The gig economy and contingent work: An occupational health assessment. *Journal of Occupational and Environmental Medicine*, 59 (4): 63–66.

van Doorn, N. (2017). Platform labour: On the gendered and racialised exploitation of low-income service work in the 'on-demand' economy. *Information, Communication & Society*, 20 (6): 898–914.

Vanhala, M. & Ritala, P. (2016). HRM practices, impersonal trust and organisational innovativeness. *Journal of Managerial Psychology*, 31 (1): 95–109.

Veen, A., Barratt, T., & Goods, C. (2020). Platform-Capital's "App-etite" for control: A labour process analysis of food-delivery work in Australia. *Work, Employment and Society*, 34 (3): 388–406.

Verweire, K., & Berghe, L. (2004). *Integrated Performance Management: A Guide to Strategy Implementation*. SAGE Publications, London.

Weil, D. (2017). How to make employment fair in an age of contracting and temp work. *Harvard Business Review*, 24 March.

Wiechers, H., Coyle-Shapiro, J.A., Lub, X.D., & Ten Have, S. (2019). Triggering psychological contract breach. In Y. Griep, & C. Cooper (Eds.), *Handbook of Research on the Psychological Contract at Work*, 272–291. Edward Elgar, Cheltenham.

Wood, A.J., & Lehdonvirta, V. (2019). *Platform Labour and Structured Antagonism: Understanding the Origins of Protest in the Gig Economy*. Paper presented at the Oxford Internet Institute Platform Economy Seminar Series, 5 March.

Wood, A.J., Graham, M., Lehdonvirta, V., & Hjorth, I. (2019). Good gig, bad gig: Autonomy and algorithmic control in the global gig economy. *Work, Employment and Society*, 33 (1): 56–57.

Xiao, S. (2019). Understanding the employment status of gig-workers in China's sharing economy era – an empirical legal study. *Asian Journal of Law and Economics*, 10 (3): 1–17.

Zeitz, G., Blau, G., & Fertig, J. (2009). Boundaryless careers and institutional resources. *International Journal of Human Resource Management*, 20 (2): 372–398.

5 The future of gig work

Key issues, solutions, and future research directions

Introduction

The discourse around the rise of the gig economy has grown exponentially during the last decade. While remaining a relatively small component of the global labour market, the vast range of scholarly, media, and policy attention focused on gig work illustrates that this new economy has grown to become an intrinsic part of our society (Bérastégui, 2021). Yet, as illustrated throughout previous chapters, the challenges and opportunities brought about by this new way of working are still intensely debated. Although welcomed by customers and some workers, the gig economy undoubtedly represents a further trend towards precarious working. By challenging existing thought regarding the nature of work, employment relationships, and the practice of management, the disruptive implications of gig work are far-reaching and warrant significant investigation. Despite this, many of these issues remain underdeveloped or unexplored across gig-economy scholarship, partly because certain research streams in this domain are still in their relative infancy, but also because the idiosyncratic dimensions of gig work are often difficult for researchers to access and examine (Kuhn & Maleki, 2017).

In this final chapter, we turn to synthesising what we see as some of the key issues to be addressed in gig work, with a particular focus on exploring potential solutions to these issues and identifying areas that future researchers may consider more closely in attempting to advance knowledge and develop the field. More specifically, we first consider the importance of establishing and maintaining sustainable work practices within the gig economy, from the perspective of both workers and platform organisations, by developing practical and realistic approaches to the most significant issues at large. From there, we focus on the ongoing classification issues that exist within the gig economy by discussing potential remedies and recent developments in what is perhaps the most widely contested debate within this

DOI: 10.4324/9780429351488-5

domain. Following this, we summarise the key challenges and uncertainties experienced by gig workers in their roles. We then conclude this chapter by looking to the future of gig work in a post-pandemic world, where recent global circumstances have placed a renewed focus on the often-troubling working conditions found in the gig economy. The issues discussed in this chapter can serve as a navigating template for the push towards a gig economy that is fair, sustainable, and transparent for all stakeholders.

Key chapter takeaways

- Attempts to regulate the gig economy to date have seen different rulings favouring either gig workers or platform organisations across jurisdictions.
- Despite being constrained by the inherent strictures of the gig-working model, there have been several reported incidences of gig workers attempting to formally and informally reclaim elements of power and autonomy in their roles, either via organised collective action or individual resistance efforts.
- Beyond potential misclassification issues, gig workers face several other uncertainties in their roles, many of which arise from the pervasiveness of algorithmic technologies in monitoring and controlling their activities.
- The lived experiences of gig workers raise significant concerns about job quality in this form of labour.
- Many gig economy sectors experienced a surge in demand throughout the COVID-19 pandemic, with many gig workers being deemed "essential", despite still lacking most basic employment protections and benefits.

Creating a sustainable gig economy

The diversity of issues associated with gig work, such as potential worker misclassification, legal issues, and the pervasiveness of technology, understandably raises questions about the long-term sustainability of this new economy. The "gig" business model benefits platform organisations by focusing on the significant reduction of labour costs at all junctures (Meijerink et al., 2021). Yet, there exists concern among the public and policymakers across the globe regarding the implications of the gig economy for the future of work. For instance, it has been argued that gig working fragments our concept of work, increases casualisation, and undermines the standard employment relationship (Wood et al., 2019). The complexities of gig work make it difficult to propose solutions as to how this fragmented working relationship can be effectively managed. The fluid, economic business model that underpins gig work means there is little regard for ensuring "fit" between worker and platform organisation, with seemingly minimal interest in worker retention on a long-term basis (Friedman, 2014). Indeed, this fluidity characterises the overall operations of many platform organisations. For example, Deliveroo withdrew from the competitive German market in 2019, ceasing operations almost overnight in a region with over 1,000 riders and just under 100 employees, because it "decided to focus on other markets" (Nicola & Lanxon, 2019). Ultimately, the fact that gig work and the platform organisations are not rooted in or embedded to a particular place means the work itself is precarious and unstable.

Perhaps the most obvious and widely discussed path to resolving the issues inherent in gig work is a legal one – in other words, revising or updating existing employment legislation to effectively govern the gig economy. It is unsurprising, then, that much scholarly literature and broader discourse on gig work has considered, at least to some extent, potential remedies to "fix" legal and policy architectures in this domain (Bonet et al., 2013; Tran & Sokas, 2017). These discussions have focused on issues such as labour exploitation, taxation, and worker classification (Prassl, 2018; Schiek & Gideon, 2018). A commonly explored solution is the proposal to create a special employment status for gig workers, acknowledging that the characteristics of these individuals do not fully comply with either the definition of employee or the self-employed (Maselli et al., 2016). The rationale is the creation of "flexicurity" for workers, signalling a type of intermediate classification that acknowledges the flexibility of gig work, while also providing some limited form of labour protection (De Stefano, 2016). The benefits brought about by such a change may well be widespread – at once, this solution potentially fills the regulatory gap affecting the gig economy, while also managing expectations by more clearly defining the specific nature of the working relationship. We explore this issue in greater depth later in this chapter.

However, the process of actually implementing a solution of this nature is far from straightforward. For example, recent years have seen a multitude of different rulings on the same issues regarding gig workers, with similar types of workers being determined as employees or independent contractors across different jurisdictions (Johnston & Land-Kazlauskas, 2018; McGaughey, 2018). With the recent example of Assembly Bill 5 and Proposition 22 in California's gig economy (see Chapter 2), it is becoming increasingly apparent that many larger platform organisations are powerful enough to persist in contesting efforts to regulate the gig economy, making it unlikely that a universal solution of this nature will be accomplished with any ease. It appears to be a case of the platform organisations wanting to change the law rather than change themselves. As a result, in the interim, it has been proposed that it is beneficial to concentrate the search to remedy some of gig working's shortcomings elsewhere, such as seeking to resolve the uniquely complex, yet less formal issues and challenges that arise between the multiple parties involved in gig work: in other words, between the gig worker, the platform organisation, and the customer (Duggan et al., 2021). Identifying and addressing the most pertinent imbalances in each of these relationships certainly appears likely to provide a useful foundation in the formation of a functional working arrangement.

To date, scholarly and grey literatures have proposed a vast range of recommendations and potential solutions for addressing the various types of challenges encountered in the gig economy and its associated work variants. Although these recommendations and solutions are highly diverse in terms of specific details, most tend to address, in some capacity, the core issues described above. In summarising the breadth and scope of the recommended solutions across existing literature, Bajwa et al. (2018) note that these may be divided into three main categories:

1. Government and public sector responses: by focusing on the development of legislative and policy-driven measures, these recommendations most commonly propose the provision of greater benefits and protections for gig workers, ranging from reclassification of employment status, to more novel and alternative potential solutions such as mobile benefits and the creation of "flexicurity."
2. Worker-led responses: this category of solutions focuses on the perspective of gig workers and the capacity of these individuals to drive change in the gig economy. With heightened coverage of gig workers' efforts to either formally unionise or create informal communities to share information and support, this category is receiving increased attention across research (McGaughey, 2018). Likewise, literature focusing on understanding the lived experiences of gig workers is currently experiencing significant growth (Jabagi et al., 2019).
3. Private sector responses: this final category focuses on the potential for platform organisations to voluntarily address the classification issues within the gig economy via more effective self-regulation. Outcomes of these responses would include the hiring of gig workers as employees and the provision of health insurance, minimum wage entitlements, and so on. However, given the lack of homogeneity across platform organisations and the specific policies and processes implemented, this category appears to be the least commonplace across existing literature.

The classification issue: regulating gig work

While the gig economy has drawn more attention and is more novel than other forms of contingent work, it can be argued as reflecting a larger trend of employers shirking their responsibilities to workers' compensation by classifying workers as independent contractors (Tran & Sokas, 2017). In Chapter 2, we identified the crucial role of technology in facilitating work in the gig economy. Building on this, we discussed how distinguishing between three different variants of gig work – app-work, crowdwork, and capital platform work – represents an important initial step towards a more coherent typology of gig workers, which, in turn, is central to better understanding the issues faced by these workers (Duggan et al., 2020). Additionally, this is also an important departure for public policymaking bodies, who are being asked to consider appropriate protections in several jurisdictions (Berg, 2016; Friedman, 2014).

Yet, despite detailed debate in recent years, the same broad question remains: how can the gig economy be most effectively regulated? As previously discussed, a commonly cited suggestion is to reclassify gig workers as employees, thereby providing the protections and benefits that accompany company employment, but eradicating the flexibility that accompanies gig work (Cappelli & Keller, 2013). In a similar vein, some scholars claim that a more effective solution could be the creation of a special status for gig workers (Taylor et al., 2017). This is in recognition that the characteristics of gig workers do not fully comply with either the definition of employees or the self-employed, but rather fall somewhere between both. This confusion is confirmed by the different rulings of different courts on the same issue (Maselli et al., 2016). For example, in November 2016, two former drivers for Uber were ruled by New York State regulators to be employees and thus eligible for unemployment payments, rather than independent contractors, as the company has maintained. However, until more recently, many of these cases tended to settle, yielding benefit for individual plaintiffs but little systemic change (Tran & Sokas, 2017)

To exacerbate the situation, regulating the gig economy is made even more complex by the fact that technology appears to be developing faster than labour regulation. According to Maselli et al. (2016), this calls for a close collaboration between researchers and policymakers, who should combine forces to further our understanding of the many advantages and challenges posed by the gig economy. Labour law and institutions urgently need to catch up to the new reality of this form of work and develop new tools to protect and enhance minimum standards for workers in digital platform organisation (Minter, 2017). In examining potential policy approaches to addressing the regulatory deficit surrounding gig work, Flanagan (2018) argues for an eclectic approach to using and strengthening legislation designed to safeguard the rights of consumers and providers of services, including contractors, and regardless of employment status. Ultimately, an important starting point in this discussion is to increase transparency, engagement, and communication between stakeholders. Direct engagement between platform organisations and workers, workers' advocates, and policymakers can help to mitigate the risks posed to labour standards by digital business models, thereby addressing regulatory gaps (Minter, 2017).

The difficulties and lengthy timeframes associated with forming and executing regulatory changes have led to the proposal of alternative, less formal approaches to implementing change. Healy et al. (2017) argue that the gig economy deserves more significant attention from the community of work and employment relations scholars, to scrutinise, critique, and add much-needed depth to the evidence available. For example, the difficulties associated with studying and measuring the gig economy have left many questions unanswered, including who exactly works in the gig economy, why they do so, and whether such participation offers a pathway into more traditional employment, or indeed, if that transition is even desired by those involved. Likewise, from the perspective of platform organisations, there are questions about optimal human resource and wage-setting practices, such as how to handle high turnover of workers and perceptions of unfair treatment (Healy et al., 2017). Elsewhere, there are also issues for employment relations scholars to contend with in attempting to theorise the gig economy, especially in terms of the power relations between "employers," workers, and consumers (Healy et al., 2017). Literature to date has struggled with this issue, identifying how established frameworks within work and employment scholarship do not readily apply to gig work without significant manipulation or expansion of conceptual boundaries.

Yet, it is also important to highlight that recent years have seen a more rapid pace of change and development in efforts to regulate the gig economy, signalling that the extensive scholarly and policy interest throughout the last decade has gained worthwhile traction. For example, in early 2021, the United Kingdom's Supreme Court ruled that Uber drivers should be categorised as workers, not contractors. This judgement meant that Uber drivers in the United Kingdom were now entitled to a minimum wage, holiday pay, and various other protections that accompany conventional employment. In explaining the reasoning behind the ruling, the Court said that the working relationship between Uber and the driver is tightly defined and controlled, with the platform organisation exerting significant control over the work of drivers and the services that they can provide (Keane, 2021). The Court also highlighted the challenges that arise from Uber imposing penalties on drivers if they turn down fares. Responding to the decision, an

Uber spokesperson said it respected the Court's decision, but that significant changes had been made to this area of the organisation's operations since the case first began in 2016. Similarly, also in early 2021, court judges in Amsterdam ruled that food-delivery workers with Deliveroo were not freelancers, and that these workers should instead be considered as staff and paid in line with the official pay and conditions agreement for the sector. Following the ruling, Deliveroo announced its intention to appeal the decision to the Dutch Supreme Court, noting that the ruling meant riders would no longer be able to choose when and for how long they wanted to work (Dutch News, 2021).

Worker resistance and collective action in the gig economy

Although literature has established that much of the power in gig-working relationships lies with the platform organisation, some limited research has also explored the potential for gig workers to collectivise in efforts to shape their conditions of work (Schiek & Gideon, 2018). Generally, there is a lack of formal worker associations or trade unions among gig workers. This, perhaps, can be largely attributed to the difficulty in collectivising a workforce which is largely geographically dispersed and working in isolation. The International Labour Organisation (2018) has pointed to the difficulties that gig workers encounter in accessing state regulatory machinery and legal frameworks. Consequently, there is an absence of collective bargaining mechanisms with digital platform organisations (De Stefano, 2016). Similarly, gig workers are also considered to be at significant structural disadvantages due to power asymmetries where the initiation of legal action can lead to their deactivation from the platform organisation, resulting in a loss of income (McGaughey, 2018). For example, Walker et al. (2021) argue that the algorithmic technologies utilised by platform organisations act as a form of "biopower" – a term associated with Foucault to describe the technological power for managing humans in large groups – in prospering fragmentation, isolation, and resignation.

Yet, despite these challenges, it is also worth highlighting that collective action is far from structurally impossible for gig workers. Existing literature suggests that gig workers as a group have made efforts to enhance their power, unionise, and have created forums to share information and hold platform organisations to account. Heeks (2017) highlights that there is evidence of some trade union activity which covers a small segment of gig workers. For example, in the United States, the Freelancers Union provides representation and support to freelancers as entrepreneurs; while in the United Kingdom, the Independent Workers Union of Great Britain

(IWGB) represents physical gig workers. However, there remains considerable scepticism concerning the existence of full-fledged collective bargaining arrangements (Johnson & Land-Kazlauskas, 2017). Various gig-worker initiatives have also been formed, generally with the goals of securing enhanced working conditions and protections. One particular initiative is the Good Work Code established by the National Domestic Workers Alliance. This code proposes core values that it envisages will act as a normative framework for platform organisations to follow (van Doorn, 2017). Other collective worker initiatives include the App-Based Drivers Association for US-based rideshare gig workers on platforms such as Uber and Lyft. To date, these initiatives have focused on negotiating improved job design and securing better conditions for gig workers.

Likewise, gig workers are increasingly engaging in collective action against platform organisations to negotiate for better employment conditions and job security (Healy et al., 2017). Like all forms of intense surveillance, algorithmic surveillance generates opportunities for worker resistance (Newlands, 2020). For example, in 2016, workers with food-delivery platform organisation Deliveroo engaged in wildcat strikes in efforts to resist organisational changes to their terms and conditions. While the changes implemented by the platform organisation claimed to achieve greater flexibility, workers were left dissatisfied with the extremely low levels of pay arising from the new payment calculation system which was introduced without consultation with workers (Schiek & Gideon, 2018; Vallas & Schor, 2020). The workers were represented by the IWGB, with Deliveroo eventually making concessions to guarantee pay for those who worked during peak hours, in addition to allowing workers to opt in rather than opt out of the reformed payment scheme. The Deliveroo strike is therefore considered an important catalyst for the collective organisation of gig workers. Strikes have subsequently taken place in countries such as Italy, Spain, Germany, and France.

Finally, research has shown that gig-worker resistance can also be more individualised and informal, where workers manage the various constraints placed upon them via everyday resilience, reworking, and resistance practices (Anwar & Graham, 2020). Similarly, Barratt, Goods, and Veen (2020) highlight how gig workers may engage in a type of entrepreneurial agency, wherein they seek to materially improve their own individual conditions, rather than directly or collectively challenge the business models of platform organisations. In describing how this resistance may materialise, Kaine and Josserand (2019) describe the potential for gig workers to develop "algorithmic competency" – a willingness to experiment, manipulate, and make sense of the algorithm – as a potential element of gig workers' repertoire of resistance. At an individual level, such resistance or disobedience may be a source of personal satisfaction for the worker, wherein the use of tacit and covert strategies demonstrates a type of informal solidarity among workers (Mulholland, 2004). This aligns with recent perspectives on how resistance is most likely to occur, and most likely to be effective, in the contemporary workplace. For example, we identify similarities with the concept of the "collective worker," wherein individuals collectively become conscious of the conditions of their oppression and exploitation at work, and informally work together to resist the iniquities of the labour process (Martinez-Lucio & Steward, 1997; Mulholland, 2004). In this scenario, resistance becomes less institutionalised and more individualised, accounting for new, modern approaches that renew the workplace as a site of struggle.

Gig workers: addressing uncertainties

The social aspects of gig work are heavily shaped by technology and digitalised management tools (Duggan et al., 2020; Meijerink & Keegan, 2019). Although the use of algorithmic management allows for increased efficiency and innovation, the lack of human representation and engagement on behalf of the platform organisation weakens social ties and forms perhaps the largest obstacle for individuals seeking to craft anything resembling a more conventional, meaningful working arrangement (Wang et al., 2020). Shanahan and Smith (2021) describe platform work as a particularly acute instance of the individualisation of economic risk, wherein labour commodification intensifies and the traits that uphold the standard employment relationship are subsumed by a novel, disruptive business model. In fact, literature has argued that gig work, in many ways, resembles a new type of unregulated, digital Taylorism (Healy et al., 2017), highlighting that the growth of gig work reflects the normalisation of what in the past constituted poor or undesirable working conditions (Myhill et al., 2021). Thus, gig work disrupts the contours of our traditional understanding of the employment relationship by introducing changes in where, how, and what work is completed for platform organisations (Bankins et al., 2020; Shanahan & Smith, 2021; Sherman & Morley, 2020).

Yet, we must also exercise caution by not assuming that the experiences of gig workers are homogenous, and we must instead work towards achieving a fuller understanding of the individual motivations and experiences of gig workers. Contrasting with discussions of algorithmic control and worker exploitation, research also tells us that, for those seeking a more casual arrangement, the heavily digitalised nature of the gig-working relationship may be more desirable by allowing increased flexibility and liberation from the confines of a traditional office environment (Allen & Berg, 2014; Ashford et al., 2018). Clearly, there is still much left unanswered and unknown in the context of understanding gig work and those who participate. However, what is known is that the very nature of this work results in many fundamental aspects of a more traditional, transparent employment relationship being enabled and delivered exclusively via digital platforms (Kuhn & Maleki, 2017). Accordingly, a key starting point in solving this issue lies in the achievement of effective, accurate communications to appropriately understand and manage the expectations of gig workers. Likewise, for platform organisations, improving transparency appears to be an important initial action in clearly defining what the gig-working relationship entails, and crucially, what it does not entail.

Algorithmic technologies and digital surveillance

A common thread in the current debate is that the proliferation of platform organisations – and perhaps more importantly, the technologies utilised by these platform organisations – have greatly impacted on both the type and quality of work available (Berg & Rani, 2018; Kashyap & Bhatai, 2018; Graham et al., 2017). The gig economy has essentially been made possible by concurrent advances in digitalisation and telecommunications. Consequently, the technologies underpinning gig work allow platform organisations to profit from labour–capital relations, while not officially acting as employers (Williams et al., 2021). Platform organisations not only allow for the remote connection of customers and contractors everywhere in the world, but also maximum standardisation of the organisation and delivery of work. By assuming duties conventionally assigned to human resources departments, algorithms are given responsibility for making the decisions that affect work, limiting human involvement in the labour process (Bérastégui, 2021). Thus, empirical research is warranted to more comprehensively understand the impact of these relatively novel and alternative digitalised management practices for workers, and indeed, for the people-management function as the workplace continues to change (Bankins & Formosa, 2020). Although offering budgetary efficiencies, it is important that a more holistic understanding of the impact of such technologies is obtained.

While gig workers often appear unclear about which data are being collected and how they are used by the platform organisation, the internalisation of the supervisory function is potent enough to create an overall climate of discipline and control. From the moment they commence their roles – perhaps even prior to this, if you take algorithmic shortlisting at the recruitment stage into account – gig workers are submerged in a complex arrangement where most managerial processes and responsibilities are reconfigured via an algorithm (Williams et al., 2021). The algorithmically enabled control and supervision found in the gig economy is uniquely distinctive, both for its encompassing and comprehensive nature, and for its ability to influence workers' motivation and perceptions of autonomy (Norlander et al., 2021). Recent studies suggest that platform organisations' algorithmic control strategies, while subtle, are diverse and comprehensive, particularly where gamification and ranking systems are utilised (Gandini, 2016; Gerber & Krzywdzinski, 2019). While these technologies may allow increased flexibility in where and when to work, the same technologies also restrict autonomy by facilitating increased monitoring of workers and reducing control over their work (Mazmanian et al., 2013). This outcome potentially renders gig workers as unable to reap the benefits expected from working virtually and remotely, while also finding themselves trapped in a state of constant precariousness, comparable to a permanent probationary period (Kalleberg & Vallas, 2018).

Consequently, the algorithmic control systems utilised by platforms organisations seemingly contradict promises of autonomy, with most of the aforementioned mechanisms designed specifically for the purposes of workforce management and enabling sophisticated control and surveillance of workers (Pichault & McKeown, 2019). There is evidence that constant monitoring and automated managerial techniques contribute to an increasingly hectic pace of work, a lack of trust towards the platform, and pronounced power asymmetries, limiting workers' opportunities to resist or develop effective forms of internal voice (Gegenhuber et al., 2020). Platform organisations' remote technologies are also redefining the boundaries between private and public space. The fear of missing out on lucrative gigs potentially leads to an obsessive relationship with the platform organisation and encourages a mindset of "always and everywhere" availability (Bérastégui, 2021), as opposed to the lure of the individual possessing full agency in deciding when and where to work.

The lived experiences of gig workers: issues with job quality

Platform organisations have expanded significantly, both in terms of international growth and the types of services offered, and are often positioned as providing considerable benefits for firms via lower employment costs, and for individuals via enhanced flexibility, autonomy, and the opportunity to diversify income streams (Adamson & Roper, 2019; Drouillard, 2017). However, in contrast to this positive narrative, there remains a wealth of debate regarding the quality of gig work (Montgomery & Baglioni, 2020). Decent work, in general, emphasises four key components: the role of governments and institutions in creating jobs with development potential; the legal protection of employee rights; opportunities for social dialogue; and work that is safe, healthy, adequately compensated, and promotes work-life balance (Ghai, 2003; Burchell et al., 2014). Based on this understanding, scholars have highlighted that there appears to be an absence of decent work in the gig economy (MacDonald & Giazitzoglu, 2019). This absence is manifested in the form of overlong working hours, very little social protection for employees, little union representation and collective voice opportunities, and the fragmentation of work processes (Tassinari & Maccarrone, 2020; Wood et al., 2018). Moreover, severe health-and-safety issues are also evident in some forms of gig work. For example, rideshare drivers have been shown to suffer from fatigue, and we also know of many cases of accidents arising from this form of work (Christie & Ward, 2019).

Consequently, there is important emerging academic debate on job quality in digital platform organisations (Spencer, 2018). Goods et al. (2019), for example, suggest that the gig economy is "a new juncture in capitalist production" and its implications for job quality need to be taken seriously by scholars and other stakeholders. We are also concerned with emerging evidence that gig workers seek to develop competencies useful in furthering their careers, and the potential lack of such opportunities within existing arrangements (Maffie, 2020; Petriglieri et al., 2018). Working in isolation is also detrimental to professional identity, as workers are shorn of role models or career mentors. Without the protective cloak of such identity, workers are more likely to experience occupational stress and to suffer from anxiety, burnout, and depression. In this regard, research shows that micro-workers represent an especially vulnerable population, their identity rendered fragile by lack of meaning (Bérastégui, 2021).

Therefore, to advance understanding of job quality in gig work, we must examine which specific characteristics either facilitate or inhibit the development of decent work. As we see it, the issue to be addressed in this regard lies in striking the balance between flexibility, sustainability, and opportunity for gig workers. Importantly, recent research demonstrates that in spite of objective observations as to the characteristics of job quality, the subjective experience of gig workers varies between platforms as well as in accordance with individual worker characteristics (e.g. those undertaking gig work as a primary or supplementary source of income) (Myhill et al., 2021).

Some platform organisations have already engaged in this debate by offering potential solutions. For example, Uber recently launched "Uber

Works," an extension of its service that connects casual workers with businesses offering short-term roles in various sectors, allowing individuals to compare pay rates and sign up for shifts that suit their schedules (Uber, 2019). Likewise, the Deliveroo Rider Academy offers workers reduced-rate access to online learning courses, apprenticeships, and mentoring opportunities to help develop their careers. However, although these initiatives are an encouraging starting point, the broader issue regarding the potential unsustainability of gig work remains (Ashford et al., 2018).

As a slight departure, there is some evidence that gig work has also started to emerge in a number of professional areas, although Minifie and Wiltshire (2016) note that it is less likely to occur in professional areas where tasks are complex, where they require deep knowledge and teamwork, and where the work must be performed on a continuous basis. However, limited research highlights that forms of gig working can be found in areas such as accounting, consulting, and legal work. This type of growth may make the gig economy a place where decent work can flourish and where arrangements can truly represent a stepping-stone for workers to get their careers started (Stewart & Owens, 2013). However, it is important to note that this potential may be due to the improved pay and conditions that traditionally accompany these professional roles, rather than representing a change in the nature of gig work itself.

The gig economy in a post-pandemic world

Discussions of labour-market challenges and growing uncertainties for workers seem particularly relevant at the time of writing, as the world grapples with and attempts to emerge from the COVID-19 pandemic. The societal implications of this global crisis pose significant and unprecedented challenges for the future of work and workplace design, especially where the need for increased remote working has come to the fore. While participation in the gig economy has grown steadily throughout the last decade, levels of demand on several platform organisations have expanded exponentially since the onset of the coronavirus pandemic (Henderson, 2020). Gig workers across various industries have, in many cases, been central to the delivery of key services during the period, while simultaneously remaining one of the most at-risk groups in the labour market by receiving little by way of social and employment benefits and protections (Griswold, 2020). For example, demand on food-delivery services skyrocketed throughout 2020, with many new restaurants signing up as more outlets had little alternative but to supply delivery services during lockdown (Healy, 2020). Similarly, for the first time in the history of the platform organisation, Uber generated more revenue from delivering food than transporting people in 2020, signifying the colossal demand for these services (Healy, 2020). Thus, the ongoing pandemic is ultimately raising important questions around the conceptualisation of what constitutes high-value and essential work.

Furthermore, the crisis has upended the traditional "nine-to-five" working world and caused many blue- and white-collar employees to pursue gig work for additional, or even primary, income during these unprecedented times (Henderson, 2020). Although demand for gig workers has accelerated since the start of the pandemic, competition for these jobs has also increased. Workers who participate in the gig economy as their sole source of income must now compete with one another, as well as previously full-time employees who have been forced into gig work (Henderson, 2020). According to Bérastégui (2021), the heightened social status of gig workers throughout the pandemic has indirectly placed a renewed focus on the extremely precarious working conditions experiences by individuals in this domain, thereby highlighting that gig workers are, in some ways, the "guinea pigs" of the new world of work. Likewise, with indications that remote working is likely to remain a core fixture in the future of work in certain domains, concerns naturally arise that some aspects of the gig economy paradigm may go mainstream and become commonplace sooner than expected. In this context, addressing workplace fragmentation and digital surveillance is even more important, with far-reaching implications that extend well beyond the realm of gig work (Bérastégui, 2021).

Conclusion

This chapter has summarised the key issues in gig work that are likely to be particularly salient for workers, platform organisations, and policymakers in the future. Our discussion has designedly focused on these issues from the perspective of gig workers for the most part, as they are at the very core of the gig economy, and also it is they who hold the most vulnerable and precarious position in the working arrangement. For example, we have consistently identified the pervasiveness of algorithmic technologies as a crucial point of importance in the study of gig work, given the capacity of these technologies to replace human supervision and to force workers to self-organise and self-motivate (Jabagi et al., 2019). Yet, ultimately, the challenges that exist for gig workers are likely to extend to platform organisations in many ways, as exemplified by consistently troubling accounts detailing the implications for workers' well-being and productivity. With high worker turnover levels and ongoing negative media attention, one imagines that the organisations at the centre of the debacle must be concerned with improving the experiences of workers, beyond engaging in such discussions as a merely nominal activity. Likewise, in the interests of creating a healthier and more sustainable social contract at work, it seems obvious that policymakers ought to be concerned with the ongoing classification issues that dominate most discourse on the gig economy, particular as such issues tend to receive widespread media coverage.

There is much scope to incorporate the perspective of platform organisations into research efforts to a greater degree than is currently evident in the literature. This, we argue, would provide a more nuanced understanding of the labour process of gig workers. Yet, achieving this is also easier said than done, with the securing of access to these organisations remaining a significant challenge for researchers. Likewise, further methodological improvements can help to progress knowledge. For example, there is a lack of insights into the experiences of gig workers over time, with both existing quantitative and qualitative data overwhelmingly representing point-in-time accounts (i.e. cross-sectional research is dominant). The use of more longitudinal research designs is arguably even more pertinent in the gig-economy context than more traditional work settings, given the rapid change and dynamism that exists. The ability to track developments over a period of time is likely to be especially useful in enabling greater and more apt theorisation on this novel form of work. Moreover, future research should also seek to build larger and more diverse samples (e.g. across geographic locations and industries) to enable wider generalisation. This is because, in many cases, the most recognisable platform organisations (e.g. Uber, Deliveroo) tend to dominate this research landscape. While calling for such advancements, we are cognisant that researching the gig economy is challenging from a methodological perspective.

Scholarship on the gig economy is undoubtedly experiencing a significant surge, which, in many ways, is unsurprising given the breadth and scope of the issues to be addressed in this domain. Research on gig work, in general, is hugely diverse in spanning multiple disciplines, perspectives, and levels of analysis. Given the rapid pace of change in the gig economy, it is important to recognise the merits of this existing research in keeping pace, more or less, with these developments. For example, huge strides have been made in more effectively conceptualising the precise nature of gig work, examining the role of algorithmic technologies, and addressing the most significant legal and ethical complexities of this form of work. Importantly, many studies, both conceptual and empirical, have sought to place the lived experiences of gig workers at the very centre of their analysis. This needs to continue in the interests of offering a way forward to address many of the challenges that arise in this dynamic form of labour.

References

Adamson, M., & Roper, I. (2019). "Good" jobs and "Bad" jobs: Contemplating job quality in different contexts. *Work, Employment and Society*, 33 (4): 551–559.

Allen, D., & Berg, C. (2014). *The Sharing Economy: How Over-Regulation Could Destroy an Economic Revolution.* Institute of Public Affairs. Melbourne, Australia.

Anwar, M.A., & Graham, M. (2020). Hidden transcripts of the gig economy: Labour agency and the new art of resistance among African gig workers. *EPA: Economy and Space*, 52 (7): 1269–1291.

Ashford, S.J., Caza, B.B., & Reid, E.M. (2018). From surviving to thriving in the gig economy: A research Agenda for individuals in the new world of work. *Research in Organizational Behavior*, 38: 23–41.

Bajwa, U., Knorr, L., Di Ruggiero, E., Gastaldo, D., & Zendel, A. (2018). *Towards an Understanding of Workers' Experiences in the Global Gig Economy.* University of Toronto, Dalla Lana School of Public Health, Toronto.

Bankins, S., & Formosa, P. (2020). When AI meets PC: Exploring the implications of workplace social robots and a human-robot psychological contract. *European Journal of Work and Organizational Psychology*, 29 (2): 215–229.

Barratt, T., Goods, C., & Veen, A. (2020). "I'm my own boss…": Active intermediation and "entrepreneurial" worker agency in the Australian gig economy. *EPA: Economy and Space*, 52 (8): 1643–1661.

Bérastégui, P. (2021). *Exposure to Psychological Risk Factors in the Gig Economy: A Systematic Review.* European Trade Union Institute. Brussels, Belgium.

Berg, J. (2016). Income security in the on-demand economy: Findings and policy lessons from a survey of crowdworkers. *ILO: Conditions of Work and Employment Series No. 74*, 1–33.

Berg, J., & Rani, U. (2018). *Digital Labour Platforms and the Future of Work: Towards Decent Work in the Online World.* International Labour Organisation, Geneva.

Bonet, R., Cappelli, P., & Hamori, M. (2013). Labour market intermediaries and the new paradigm for human resources. *Academy of Management Annals*, 7 (1): 341–392.

Burchell, B., Sehnbruch, K., Piasna, A., & Agloni, N. (2014). The quality of employment and decent work: Definitions, methodologies, and ongoing debates. *Cambridge Journal of Economics*, 38 (2): 459–477.

Cappelli, P., & Keller, J.R. (2013). Classifying work in the new economy. *Academy of Management Review*, 38 (4): 575–596.

Christie, N., & Ward, H. (2019). The health and safety risks for people who drive for work in the gig economy, *Journal of Transport & Health*, 13, 115–127.

De Stefano, V. (2016). The rise of the "just-in-time" workforce: On-demand work, crowdwork and labour protection in the gig economy. *International Labour Office: Conditions of Work and Employment Series*, 71.

Drouillard, M. (2017). Addressing Voids: How Digital Start-ups in Kenya Create Market Infrastructure. In: Ndemo B., Weiss T. (eds) Palgrave Studies of Entrepreneurship in Africa, 97–131. Palgrave Macmillan, London.

Duggan, J., Sherman, U., Carbery, R., & McDonnell, A. (2020). Algorithmic management and app-work in the gig economy: A research agenda for employment relations and HRM. *Human Resource Management Journal*, 30 (1): 114–132.

Duggan, J., Sherman, U., Carbery, R., & McDonnell, A. (2021). Multi-party working relationships in gig work: Towards a new perspective. In: V. Daskalova, G. Jansen, & J. Meijerink (Eds.), *Platform Economy Puzzles: A Multidisciplinary Perspective on Gig Work*. Edward Elgar, in press.

Dutch News (2021). Deliveroo to appeal to Supreme Court after judges say riders are not freelancers. *DutchNews.nl*, 17 February.

Flanagan, F. (2018). Theorising the gig economy and home-based service work. *Journal of Industrial Relations*, 61 (1): 57–78.

Friedman, G. (2014). Workers without employers: Shadow corporations and the rise of the gig economy. *Review of Keynesian Economics*, 2 (2): 171–188.

Gandini, A. (2018). Labour process theory and the gig economy. *Human Relations*, 72 (6): 1039–1056.

Gegenhuber, T., Ellmer, M., & Schubler, E. (2020). Microphones, not megaphones: Functional crowdworker voice regimes on digital work platforms. *Human Relations*, in press.

Gerber, C., & Krzywdzinski, M. (2019). Brave new digital work? New forms of performance control in crowdwork. In S.P. Vallas & A. Kovalainen (Eds.), *Work and Labor in the Digital Age (Research in the Sociology of Work*, 33): 121–143. Bingley, Emerald Publishing.

Ghai, D. (2003). Decent work: Concept and indicators. *International Labour Review*, 142, 113.

Goods, C., Veen, A., & Barratt, T. (2019). "Is your gig any good?" Analysing job quality in the Australian platform-based food-delivery sector. *Journal of Industrial Relations*, 61 (4): 502–527.

Graham, M., Hjorth, I., & Lehdonvirta, V. (2017). Digital labour and development: Impacts of global digital labour platforms and the gig economy on worker livelihood. *Transfer*, 23 (2): 135–162.

Griswold, A. (2020). The month the entire world signed up for delivery. *Quartz*, 19 April.

Healy, A. (2020). Food-delivery services see Covid-related surge. *Irish Examiner*, 7 August.

Healy, J., Nicholson, D., & Pekarek, A. (2017). Should we take the gig economy seriously? *Labour and Industry: A Journal of the Social and Economic Relations of Work*, 27 (3): 232–248.

Heeks, R. (2017). *Decent Work and the Digital gig Economy: A Developing Country Perspective on Employment Impacts and Standards in Online Outsourcing, Crowdwork, etc.* Development Informatics Working Paper, 71.

Henderson, R. (2020). How COVID-19 has transformed the gig economy. *Forbes*, 10 December.

International Labour Organisation (2018). *Decent Work*. Report of the Director General. ILO, Geneva.

Jabagi, N., Croteau, A.M., Audebrand, L.K., & Marsan, J. (2019). Gig workers' motivation: Thinking beyond carrots and sticks. *Journal of Managerial Psychology*, 34 (4): 192–213.

Johnston, H., & Land-Kazlauskas, C. (2018). *Organising On-Demand: Representation, Voice, and Collective Bargaining in the Gig Economy.* Conditions of Work and Employment Series No 94. Geneva, International Labour Office.

Kaine, S., & Josserand, E. (2019). The organisation and experience of work in the gig economy. *Journal of Industrial Relations*, 61 (4): 479–501.

Kalleberg, A.L., & Vallas, S.P. (2018). Probing precarious work: Theory, research, and politics. *Precarious Work: Research in the Sociology of Work*, 31: 1–30.

Kashyap, R., & Bhatia, A. (2018). Taxi drivers and taxidars: A case study of Uber and Ola in Delhi. *Journal of Developing Societies*, 34 (2): 169–194.

Keane, J. (2021). UK Supreme Court says Uber drivers should not be classified as contractors. *Forbes*, 19 February.

Kuhn, K.M., & Maleki, A. (2017). Micro-entrepreneurs, dependent contractors, and Instaserfs: Understanding online labour platform workforces. *Academy of Management Perspectives*, 31 (3): 183–200.

MacDonald, R., & Giazitzoglu, A. (2019). Youth, enterprise and precarity: O, what is, and what is wrong with, the "gig economy"? *Journal of Sociology*, 55 (4): 724–740.

Maffie, M.D. (2020). The role of digital communities in organising gig workers. *Industrial Relations: A Journal of Economy and Society*, 59 (1): 123–149.

Martinez-Lucio, M., & Stewart, P. (1997). The paradox of contemporary labour process theory: The rediscovery of labour and disappearance of collectivism. *Capital and Class*, 21 (2): 49–77.

Maselli, I., Lenaerts, K., & Beblavy, M. (2016). Five things we need to know about the on-demand economy. *Centre for European Policy Studies*, 21.

Mazmanian, M., Orlikowski, W.J., & Yates, J. (2013). The autonomy paradox: The implications of mobile email devices for knowledge professionals. *Organization Science*, 24 (5): 1337–1357.

McGaughey, E. (2018). Taylorooism: When network technology meets corporate power. *Industrial Relations Journal*, 49 (5–6): 459–472.

Meijerink, J., & Keegan, A. (2019). Conceptualizing human resource management in the gig economy: Toward a platform ecosystem perspective. *Journal of Managerial Psychology*, 34 (4): 214–232.

Meijerink, J., Keegan, A., & Bondarouk, T. (2021). Having their cake and eating it too? Online labour platforms and human resource management as a case of institutional complexity. *International Journal of Human Resource Management*, in press.

Minifie, J., & Wiltshire, T. (2016). *Peer to Peer Pressure: Policy for the Sharing Economy* Grattan Institute, Victoria, Australia. (No. 2016–7).

Minter, K. (2017). Negotiating labour standards in the gig economy: Airtasker and union NSW. *Economic and Labour Relations Review*, 28 (3): 438–454.

Montgomery, T., & Baglioni, S. (2020). Defining the gig economy: Platform capitalism and the reinvention of precarious work. *International Journal of Sociology and Social Policy*.

Mulholland, K. (2004). Workplace resistance in an Irish call centre: Slammin', scammin', smokin', and leavin'. *Work, Employment and Society*, 18 (4): 709–724.

Myhill, K., Richards, J., & Sang, K. (2021). Job quality, fair work and gig work: The lived experiences of gig workers. *International Journal of Human Resource Management*, in press.

Newlands, G. (2020). Algorithmic surveillance in the gig economy: The organisation of work through Lefebvrian conceived space. *Organization Studies*, in press.

Nicola, S., & Lanxon, N. (2019). Amazon-backed Deliveroo pulls out of Germany in abrupt retreat. *Bloomberg Technology*, 12 August.

Norlander, P., Jukic, N., Varma, A., & Nestorov, S. (2021). The effects of technological supervision on gig workers: Organisational control and motivation of Uber, taxi and limousine drivers. *International Journal of Human Resource Management*, in press.

Petriglieri, G., Ashford, S.J., & Wrzesniewski, A. (2018). Agony and ecstasy in the gig economy: Cultivating holding environments for precarious and personalized work identities. *Administrative Science Quarterly*, 64 (1): 124–170.

Pichault, F., & McKeown, T. (2019). Autonomy at work in the gig economy: Analysing work status, content and conditions of independent professionals, *New Technology, Work and Employment*, 34 (1): 59–72.

Prassl, J. (2018). *Humans as a Service*. Oxford University Press, Oxford.

Schiek, D., & Gideon, A. (2018). Outsmarting the gig-economy through collective bargaining – EU competition law as a barrier to smart cities. *International Review of Law, Computers & Technology*, 32 (2–3), 275–294.

Shanahan, G., & Smith, M. (2021). Fair's fair: Psychological contracts and power in platform work. *International Journal of Human Resource Management*, in press.

Sherman, U.P., & Morley, M.J. (2020). What do we measure and how do we elicit it? The case for the use of repertory grid techniques in multi-party psychological contract research. *European Journal of Work and Organizational Psychology*, 29 (2): 230–242.

Spencer, D.A. (2018). Fear and hope in an age of mass automation: Debating the future of work. *New Technology, Work and Employment*, 33 (1): 1–12.

Stewart, A., & Owens, R.J. (2013). *Experience or Exploitation?: The Nature, Prevalence and Regulation of Unpaid Work Experience, Internships and Trial Periods in Australia*. University of Adelaide, Adelaide.

Tassinari, A., & Maccarrone, V. (2020). Riders on the storm: Workplace solidarity among gig economy couriers in Italy and the UK. *Work, Employment and Society*, 34 (1): 35–54.

Taylor, M., Marsh, G., Nicol, D. & Broadbent, P. (2017). *Good Work: The Taylor Review of Modern Working Practices*. Department of Business, Energy and Industrial, London.

Tran, M., & Sokas, R.K. (2017). The gig economy and contingent work: An occupational health assessment. *Journal of Occupational and Environmental Medicine*, 59 (4): 63–66.

Uber (2019). Uber works officially launched in Chicago. *Uber Technologies*, 2 October.

Vallas, S., & Schor, J.B. (2020). What do platforms do? Understanding the gig economy. *Annual Review of Sociology*, 46.

van Doorn, N. (2017). Platform labour: On the gendered and racialised exploitation of low-income service work in the "on-demand" economy. *Information, Communication & Society*, 20 (6): 898–914.

Walker, M., Fleming, P., & Berti, M. (2021). "You can't pick up a phone and talk to someone": How algorithms function as biopower in the gig economy. *Organization*, 28 (1): 26–43.

Wang, B., Liu, Y., & Parker, S.K. (2020). How does the use of information communication technology affect individuals: A work design perspective. *Academy of Management Annals*, 14: 695–725.

Williams, P., McDonald, P., & Mayes, R. (2021). Recruitment in the gig economy: Attraction and selection on digital platforms. *International Journal of Human Resource Management*, in press.

Wood, A.J., Lehdonvirta, V., & Graham, M. (2018). Workers of the internet unite? Online freelancer organisation among remote gig economy workers in six Asian and African countries. *New Technology, Work and Employment*, 33 (2): 95–112.

Wood, A.J., Graham, M., Lehdonvirta, V., & Hjorth, I. (2019). Good gig, bad gig: Autonomy and algorithmic control in the global gig economy. *Work, Employment and Society*, 33 (1): 56–57.

Index

gig economy 2–3, 86–87; and algorithmic management 72–73; career issues in 78–80; and contingent work 25–26; digital platform organisations and 44–45; emergence of the 1–2, 4–5; employment legislation and 88; independent contractors and 3; long-term sustainability of 87–89; loss of earnings 3; and low-skilled jobs 3; as a new phenomenon 1; organisations 1; other terms for 5; overview of 14–15; performance management 68, 69, 75; post-COVID pandemic 98–99; recommended solutions to issues in 89; as a research area 13; technology in 44; typical offerings 2; what is different about it 5–6; workers collective action in the 92–94

gig work: advantages of 8–9; algorithmic recording and 58; algorithmic replacing and 58–59; algorithmic technologies and 12, 66; app-work 29–31; classification issues in 36–37; classification of 12, 29, 34; conceptualisations of 20–21; as contingent labour 37; disadvantages of 9; disruptive nature of 66, 67–69; employment relations issues and 74–76; forms of 29, 38; heterogeneity of **37**; independent contractors status of 10–11; issues in 99–100; multi-party working relationship in 80; multi-relationships in 67–69; regulating 90; role of technology in 60; and technological trends impact on 47–48

gig work forms, based on digital platform organisations 1

gig work literature 10; classification of gig work in 10–11

gig workers 44; algorithmic management of 50–51; algorithmic technologies and 87; career issues for 78–80; classification of 88, 90–92; COVID-19 pandemic and 87; customer evaluation and 73–74; denial of employment status of 75; employment status of 79; evaluation of 76; experiences of 12–13, 38, 74–80, 94; health and safety of 7; job autonomy 76–78, 80; lived experiences of 12–14, 66, 68, 80, 87, 89, 96–98; and power asymmetries 51–52; relationship with the platform organisations and 71–72; social protections for 47, 50–51; statistics about 7–8; the uncertainties of gig work and 94–95; understanding 3–4

gig-worker initiatives 93

gig-worker resistance 93

gig-working arrangement/relationships 8; the customer and 73–74; and platform organisations 72–73

global economic crisis 4

global financial crisis 8

global labour market, gig economy and 86

Good Work Code 93

Goods, C. 93

Handy 2

Healy, J. 91

Heeks, R. 92

hierarchical reporting relationships, and the gig economy 9

host conventions 36

Howcroft, D. 34, **38**

human interaction 9, 48, 79

human-centred management 78

hyper-individualism 25

independent contractors: algorithmic replacing and 58–59; Assembly Bill 5 (AB5) and 36; in the gig economy 3; gig workers as 10–11; misclassification 12; monitoring of 48; self-employed 25; self-management and 78

Independent Workers Union of Great Britain (IWGB) 92

individual workers, and court rulings 75

International Labour Organisation 92

invisible workers 12, 48

Ivanova, M. 57

IWGB (Independent Workers Union of Great Britain) 92

Jago, A.S. 73

job autonomy, of gig workers 76–78, 80